DO Drops
Volume 10

DO Drops
Volume 10

Daily Bible Devotional

Dr. Bo Wagner

Word of His Mouth Publishers
Mooresboro, NC

All Scripture quotations are taken from the **King James Version** of the Bible.

ISBN: 978-1-941039-41-0
Printed in the United States of America
©2023 Dr. Bo Wagner

Word of His Mouth Publishers
Mooresboro, NC
www.wordofhismouth.com

Cover art by Chip Nuhrah

Devotion 1

The book of Ezra picks up where the book of 2 Chronicles leaves off. The seventy-year captivity is over, Nebuchadnezzar is long since dead, and Babylon has fallen to the Medes and the Persians. Cyrus, the king of the Persians, is commissioning the children of Israel to go back to their homeland and rebuild the temple of God. Ezra, the priest, will be the central figure in the book that bears his name. The books of Ezra, Esther, and Nehemiah give us the accounts of the children of Israel still living in that part of the world after the Babylonian captivity had ended.

Ezra 1:1 *Now in the first year of Cyrus king of Persia, that the word of the LORD by the mouth of Jeremiah might be fulfilled, the LORD stirred up the spirit of Cyrus king of Persia, that he made a proclamation throughout all his kingdom, and put it also in writing, saying,* **2** *Thus saith Cyrus king of Persia, The LORD God of heaven hath given me all the kingdoms of the earth; and he hath charged me to build him an house at Jerusalem, which is in Judah.* **3** *Who is there among you of all his people? his God be with him, and let him go up to Jerusalem, which is in Judah, and build the house of the LORD God of Israel, (he is the God,) which is in Jerusalem.*

These words are nearly identical to the closing words of the book of 2 Chronicles. The house of God in Jerusalem had been destroyed many decades earlier, but God would not leave it that way. He has always had a literal, physical place for His people to come together and worship. Old Testament or New

Testament, Jew or Christian, temple or church, there has never been and never will be a time when God does not expect His people to assemble together for worship. It was so important to Him that He stirred up the spirit of Cyrus, king of Persia, to send people back to the rubble of Jerusalem and rebuild the house of worship.

And all of this is just another thing that makes the "we don't go to church; we are the church" crowd so different from God's actual expectations.

DO understand that God prizes corporate worship; He loves for all of His people to assemble together in the house of God!

Personal Notes:

_____

_____

_____

_____

_____

_____

_____

_____

_____

_____

_____

_____

_____

_____

_____

_____

_____

Devotion 2

The decree from King Cyrus had gone forth. Any Jew who wished to go was encouraged to go back to Jerusalem and rebuild the house of God. The next few verses show that process beginning to happen.

Ezra 1:5 *Then rose up the chief of the fathers of Judah and Benjamin, and the priests, and the Levites, with all them whose spirit God had raised, to go up to build the house of the LORD which is in Jerusalem.* **6** *And all they that were about them strengthened their hands with vessels of silver, with gold, with goods, and with beasts, and with precious things, beside all that was willingly offered.* **7** *Also Cyrus the king brought forth the vessels of the house of the LORD, which Nebuchadnezzar had brought forth out of Jerusalem, and had put them in the house of his gods;* **8** *Even those did Cyrus king of Persia bring forth by the hand of Mithredath the treasurer, and numbered them unto Sheshbazzar, the prince of Judah.*

The people who were looked to as leaders, the chief men of the tribes of Judah and Benjamin, rose to the occasion. They determined to go to a place that most of them had never been to build a house of God that most of them had never seen. Others around them were moved to provide for that need financially. But perhaps most remarkably, Cyrus, king of Persia, sent to his treasury and had all the vessels of the house of God that had once been in the house of God at Jerusalem brought out and given to the people who were going home. These were silver and gold vessels, for the most part; Cyrus was giving up a large chunk of wealth to do this.

How remarkable is it that God could move in the heart of people to give up comfort and wealth and security in order to work for Him! But it has always been this way; any good work of God will be birthed out of sacrifice, not convenience.

Does the work of God mean something to you? Then DO sacrifice for it!

Personal Notes:

_____

_____

_____

_____

_____

_____

_____

_____

_____

_____

_____

_____

_____

_____

_____

_____

_____

_____

_____

_____

_____

_____

Devotion 3

The Children of Israel were coming home; the temple was going to be rebuilt. And, remarkably, some things that had been in the original Temple that Nebuchadnezzar destroyed were actually still accounted for and were going to go home as well.

Ezra 1:9 *And this is the number of them: thirty chargers of gold, a thousand chargers of silver, nine and twenty knives,* **10** *Thirty basons of gold, silver basons of a second sort four hundred and ten, and other vessels a thousand.* **11** *All the vessels of gold and of silver were five thousand and four hundred. All these did Sheshbazzar bring up with them of the captivity that were brought up from Babylon unto Jerusalem.*

Five thousand four hundred vessels of gold and silver had somehow been kept in the treasury of Babylon and then Persia when Babylon fell to the Medes and Persians, and it was now going back home to Jerusalem. They were not melted down along the way; they were not captured by some other foreign power; they were not traded for goods or services. The Jews had lost much due to their disobedience, but in the mercy of God, they had not lost everything. They would have to build a new temple, but they still had some of the vessels from the old temple.

Did they deserve that? No, they did not deserve so much as a single spoon to be reserved for them. But do we deserve any of the mercy of God in our lives, either? I think you know the answer to that.

DO know that God is a holy and a just God, and the law of sowing and reaping is still in effect. But DO know also that God is a gracious and a merciful God who holds many things in store for us all during the days of our disobedience in anticipation of the eventual day of our repentance and restoration!

Personal Notes:

_____
_____
_____
_____
_____
_____
_____
_____
_____
_____
_____
_____
_____
_____
_____
_____
_____
_____
_____
_____
_____
_____
_____
_____
_____

Devotion 4

More than seventy years after the Babylonian captivity had begun, and forty-eight years after the temple had been reduced to a pile of smoking rubble, the Jews were now being allowed to go home and rebuild that temple. But to say that things had changed drastically would be an understatement. And one of the most drastic parts of that change is seen in a very subtle word in the text of Scripture.

Ezra 2:1 *Now these are the children of the province that went up out of the captivity, of those which had been carried away, whom Nebuchadnezzar the king of Babylon had carried away unto Babylon, and came again unto Jerusalem and Judah, every one unto his city;*

Province. The Jews are referred to here as children of the province, and that word refers to their home country. A province, in this case, is just a piece of land that is a tributary to another power. They were getting to go home, but home was now a province when it used to be something very different:

2 Samuel 5:12 *And David perceived that the LORD had established him king over Israel, and that he had exalted his kingdom for his people Israel's sake.*

They were once a kingdom; they were now just a province. Was it great to be going home? Absolutely. But would it have been far better not to lose their kingdom status to begin with? Absolutely. But sin often costs us things that take a very long while to regain, if ever.

DO realize that there is nothing more costly in life than sin!

Personal Notes:

_____

_____

_____

_____

_____

_____

_____

_____

_____

_____

_____

_____

_____

_____

_____

_____

_____

_____

_____

_____

_____

_____

_____

_____

_____

Devotion 5

Ezra 2, one of the longest chapters in Scripture at seventy verses, gives an enumeration of the people that came back to the land at this, the first of three returns from captivity. Verse sixty-four tells us that there were 42,360 of them. Adding in the singers, Ezra 2:65 brings the number to 50,000. But it is some of the small details given as specifics in this chapter that are so instructive.

Ezra 2:21 *The children of Bethlehem, an hundred twenty and three.*

Bethlehem was the hometown of David, their greatest king. And yet we here find just one hundred twenty-three from that town going back home. Their past glory could never translate into present protection against the effects of disobedience.

Ezra 2:23 *The men of Anathoth, an hundred twenty and eight.*

Anathoth was one of the greatest cities of the tribe of Benjamin. But the men of that town were also the ones who brutally persecuted Jeremiah the prophet. Because of that, in Jeremiah 11:23, God promised to ruin them. And the numbers coming back in captivity show that He did.

DO think far beyond the here and now as you make your decisions for the here and now because your decisions for the here and now have consequences, good or bad, that reach far beyond the here and now!

Personal Notes:

_____

_____

_____

_____

_____

_____

_____

_____

_____

_____

_____

_____

_____

_____

_____

_____

_____

_____

_____

_____

_____

_____

_____

_____

_____

_____

_____

_____

_____

Devotion 6

The Jews were going home and were going to reestablish, as best as they could, normal life and worship. But normal life and worship, for them, was contingent upon one very important thing: an accurate genealogy. The tribes were to be distinct, and families within the tribes were to be accurately recorded, especially with the tribe of Levi and the family of Aaron, out of which came the priesthood. But after decades away from home, two groups of people, it seems, had a "paperwork issue."

Ezra 2:59 *And these were they which went up from Telmelah, Telharsa, Cherub, Addan, and Immer: but they could not shew their father's house, and their seed, whether they were of Israel:* **60** *The children of Delaiah, the children of Tobiah, the children of Nekoda, six hundred fifty and two.* **61** *And of the children of the priests: the children of Habaiah, the children of Koz, the children of Barzillai; which took a wife of the daughters of Barzillai the Gileadite, and was called after their name:* **62** *These sought their register among those that were reckoned by genealogy, but they were not found: therefore were they, as polluted, put from the priesthood.*

It may seem exceedingly odd to us, in our day, to have matters both of land and of religion so dependent on a genealogy. But when you think about it, a beautiful truth emerges; God prizes the family.

The traditional, nuclear family (man and wife get married and, if God so allows, have children) is a concept that more and more is despised and denigrated in our day. Words like "patriarchal" get thrown around as if they are clumps of mud with which to dirty those who still believe in such things. But the family is still the building block of every strong society, and the more our society moves away from it, the weaker we will become, not stronger.

DO prize both the concept of the family in general, and your particular family in specific!

Personal Notes:

_____

_____

_____

_____

_____

_____

_____

_____

_____

_____

_____

_____

_____

_____

_____

_____

_____

_____

_____

_____

_____

_____

Devotion 7

The return from Persia to Jerusalem had taken place in the spring. Ezra 3 picks up the story in the early fall after the people had spent some time constructing hasty shelters in which to live and from which to do the work.

Ezra 3:1 *And when the seventh month was come, and the children of Israel were in the cities, the people gathered themselves together as one man to Jerusalem. 2 Then stood up Jeshua the son of Jozadak, and his brethren the priests, and Zerubbabel the son of Shealtiel, and his brethren, and builded the altar of the God of Israel, to offer burnt offerings thereon, as it is written in the law of Moses the man of God. 3 And they set the altar upon his bases; for fear was upon them because of the people of those countries: and they offered burnt offerings thereon unto the LORD, even burnt offerings morning and evening.*

The temple was still lying in ruins; there was no "house of God" yet for them to worship in. They were specifically sent back to build that temple, but before they even did so, they built an altar to offer burnt offerings on. In other words, though their primary task was to build a house of God, they knew they could never do so successfully without God Himself being involved. So they built an altar on which to worship Him as they began the process of building His house.

Every child of God in our day ought to be intent on "building" the house of God, the church. We ought to be intent on building the membership and the mission work and the finances and everything that goes along with a church. But if we are going to do anything for God, it will have to be God doing it through us. That being the case, start with the altar; start with prayer and worship.

DO work for God, but DO pray and worship before you ever start that work each day!

Personal Notes:

_____

_____

_____

_____

_____

_____

_____

_____

_____

_____

_____

_____

_____

_____

_____

_____

_____

_____

_____

_____

_____

Devotion 8

The remnant returned from captivity was back in the land, and they were there because of Cyrus' decree that the temple should be rebuilt. They quickly built an altar and reestablished right worship in the land. And as far as "building projects" go, that was by far the easiest task, since a simple dirt/rock altar is not too big and not too complicated. But what is pretty impressive is the time line given in starting the building of the new temple from the ground up.

Ezra 3:6 *From the first day of the seventh month began they to offer burnt offerings unto the LORD. But the foundation of the temple of the LORD was not yet laid. 7 They gave money also unto the masons, and to the carpenters; and meat, and drink, and oil, unto them of Zidon, and to them of Tyre, to bring cedar trees from Lebanon to the sea of Joppa, according to the grant that they had of Cyrus king of Persia. 8 Now in the second year of their coming unto the house of God at Jerusalem, in the second month, began Zerubbabel the son of Shealtiel, and Jeshua the son of Jozadak, and the remnant of their brethren the priests and the Levites, and all they that were come out of the captivity unto Jerusalem; and appointed the Levites, from twenty years old and upward, to set forward the work of the house of the LORD.*

They arrived and built the altar in the seventh month of that first year. They began construction on the temple in the second month of the second year, just seven months later. Even today, deciding to build a major structure usually takes years before the first shovel full of dirt is even moved. To have them begin the process just seven months after arriving from a foreign country was amazingly fast. And there is a great lesson in that.

When it comes to what we do for God and His house, procrastination ought to be regarded as one of the worst of sins. Yet believers often give lip-service to getting up and following God while not giving "hip-service" to actually doing so.

Do you know what God expects of you as a believer? Then get up and DO it, and DO it right away!

Personal Notes:

_____

_____

_____

_____

_____

_____

_____

_____

_____

_____

_____

_____

_____

_____

_____

_____

_____

_____

_____

Devotion 9

The decree of Cyrus was now becoming a reality; the foundations for the new temple were finally being laid. But the scene at that moment was perhaps the greatest scene of mixed emotions in human history.

Ezra 3:10 *And when the builders laid the foundation of the temple of the LORD, they set the priests in their apparel with trumpets, and the Levites the sons of Asaph with cymbals, to praise the LORD, after the ordinance of David king of Israel.* **11** *And they sang together by course in praising and giving thanks unto the LORD; because he is good, for his mercy endureth for ever toward Israel. And all the people shouted with a great shout, when they praised the LORD, because the foundation of the house of the LORD was laid.* **12** *But many of the priests and Levites and chief of the fathers, who were ancient men, that had seen the first house, when the foundation of this house was laid before their eyes, wept with a loud voice; and many shouted aloud for joy:* **13** *So that the people could not discern the noise of the shout of joy from the noise of the weeping of the people: for the people shouted with a loud shout, and the noise was heard afar off.*

There were young people that day who had never had a temple; they were overjoyed at this very modest temple that was being laid out. To them, it was the greatest thing ever. But there were also very old people there that day who, long ago as children, had actually seen the glorious temple of Solomon before it was destroyed. To them, the new temple was heartbreaking because it was nowhere near the glory of what they had lost.

So which view was "correct?" In this case, both. Those who never had a temple had every reason to rejoice at what they were being given, and those who had experienced Solomon's temple had every reason to mourn over what they had lost.

It will often be like this with our human emotions; some will weep, and some will rejoice over the exact same thing. So, while never wavering on right or wrong, DO be willing both to have your own emotions on an issue while also respecting the emotions of others on that same issue!

Personal Notes:

_____

_____

_____

_____

_____

_____

_____

_____

_____

_____

_____

_____

_____

_____

_____

_____

_____

Devotion 10

Once the building of the temple was underway, an offer of "help" came in. It is interesting to see how the Jews responded and why.

Ezra 4:1 *Now when the adversaries of Judah and Benjamin heard that the children of the captivity builded the temple unto the LORD God of Israel;* **2** *Then they came to Zerubbabel, and to the chief of the fathers, and said unto them, Let us build with you: for we seek your God, as ye do; and we do sacrifice unto him since the days of Esarhaddon king of Assur, which brought us up hither.* **3** *But Zerubbabel, and Jeshua, and the rest of the chief of the fathers of Israel, said unto them, Ye have nothing to do with us to build an house unto our God; but we ourselves together will build unto the LORD God of Israel, as king Cyrus the king of Persia hath commanded us.*

When the ten tribes of the Northern kingdom were carried by Assyria away many years earlier, the Assyrians repopulated the land with other people who then intermarried with the few Jews who remained, creating an entirely new race of people, the Samaritans. Interestingly, secular history gives testimony to all of this on the annals of Esar-haddon that is currently in the British Museum.

The new race of people maintained the name of the old Jewish religion but did not really know and serve and obey the God of that religion. Their offer for "help," then, was never going to work out well and was rightly refused. They could have quickly been a much bigger body of worshipers if they had accepted that

24

help, but bigger and better are not always the same thing.

Think of it this way: having a "church" built by Baptists and Jehovah's Witnesses and Mormons would be a predictable disaster! They all claim the name of Christian, but they all mean very different things by that.

DO be more intent on building right than on building big!

Personal Notes:

_____

_____

_____

_____

_____

_____

_____

_____

_____

_____

_____

_____

_____

_____

_____

_____

_____

_____

_____

_____

Devotion 11

The Samaritans came and asked to be allowed to help with the building of the temple, and to be a part of all that went on within it. They claimed to be worshipping the same God. But when they were rejected, it very quickly became apparent just how fake their supposed devotion to God really was.

Ezra 4:4 *Then the people of the land weakened the hands of the people of Judah, and troubled them in building,* **5** *And hired counsellors against them, to frustrate their purpose, all the days of Cyrus king of Persia, even until the reign of Darius king of Persia.* **6** *And in the reign of Ahasuerus, in the beginning of his reign, wrote they unto him an accusation against the inhabitants of Judah and Jerusalem.*

The philosophy of these so-called worshippers of God from Samaria was, "If we can't have it, you can't either." Mind you, they could easily have worshipped God and built temples and other places of worship right in their own towns, but they refused to be satisfied by that. So they started messing with the political process to stop the building of the temple. Cyrus, who issued the decree, was often away at war, and his wicked son, Cambyses, who hated the Jews and their God, was there to call the shots in his absence. Long story short, they managed to cause a twenty-year delay in the building of the temple.

Here is a good rule of thumb to remember. If people are only your friends when they get their way, they were never your friends to begin with. And this is especially important to remember in the context of the house of God. Be very wary of people who are proud rather than humble, and self-absorbed rather than selfless. No matter how pious people sound, if they are not still for you when they do not get their way, they likely never were.

DO be discerning!

Personal Notes:

_____

_____

_____

_____

_____

_____

_____

_____

_____

_____

_____

_____

_____

_____

_____

_____

_____

_____

_____

_____

_____

_____

_____

Devotion 12

The Samaritans, having been rebuffed in their attempt to be a part of the rebuilding of the temple, determined instead to prevent it from ever being built. It was a classic case of, "If we can't play, we will take our ball and go home!" But the damage they did was far greater than just the breaking up of a ballgame...

Ezra 4:11 *This is the copy of the letter that they sent unto him, even unto Artaxerxes the king; Thy servants the men on this side the river, and at such a time.* **12** *Be it known unto the king, that the Jews which came up from thee to us are come unto Jerusalem, building the rebellious and the bad city, and have set up the walls thereof, and joined the foundations.* **13** *Be it known now unto the king, that, if this city be builded, and the walls set up again, then will they not pay toll, tribute, and custom, and so thou shalt endamage the revenue of the kings.*

There are a couple of things to notice here. The smaller thing to notice is the usage of the word Jews. That name was almost never used prior to this time. But since it was mostly people from the tribe of Judah who came home from captivity, it became the most common name to denote any one of Israel and has been used that way extensively even up unto our day. The bigger thing to notice, though, is their assertion that Jerusalem was a "rebellious and bad city." The problem with that accusation was that it was absolutely true and that they had historical proof of it:

Ezra 4:14 *Now because we have maintenance from the king's palace, and it was not meet for us to*

28

see the king's dishonour, therefore have we sent and certified the king; **15** *That search may be made in the book of the records of thy fathers: so shalt thou find in the book of the records, and know that this city is a rebellious city, and hurtful unto kings and provinces, and that they have moved sedition within the same of old time: for which cause was this city destroyed.*

The enemy did not have to lie about Jerusalem; they were able to stop the work simply by telling the truth about its rebellious and wicked past.

DO understand that everything you do today will impact you, and even your family, well into the future!

Personal Notes:

_____

_____

_____

_____

_____

_____

_____

_____

_____

_____

_____

_____

_____

_____

_____

_____

_____

_____

Devotion 13

Having pointed the Persian authorities toward the rebellious and fickle nature of Jerusalem in years gone by, those authorities went and searched through official records to see what was there.

Ezra 4:17 *Then sent the king an answer unto Rehum the chancellor, and to Shimshai the scribe, and to the rest of their companions that dwell in Samaria, and unto the rest beyond the river, Peace, and at such a time. 18 The letter which ye sent unto us hath been plainly read before me. 19 And I commanded, and search hath been made, and it is found that this city of old time hath made insurrection against kings, and that rebellion and sedition have been made therein. 20 There have been mighty kings also over Jerusalem, which have ruled over all countries beyond the river; and toll, tribute, and custom, was paid unto them. 21 Give ye now commandment to cause these men to cease, and that this city be not builded, until another commandment shall be given from me. 22 Take heed now that ye fail not to do this: why should damage grow to the hurt of the kings? 23 Now when the copy of king Artaxerxes' letter was read before Rehum, and Shimshai the scribe, and their companions, they went up in haste to Jerusalem unto the Jews, and made them to cease by force and power. 24 Then ceased the work of the house of God which is at Jerusalem. So it ceased unto the second year of the reign of Darius king of Persia.*

In the last devotion, we focused on the fact that past wickedness caused the Jews present problems.

But in this one, please notice a bit of something different. In verse twenty, the Persian authorities stated that their own records indicated that there had been mighty kings over Jerusalem. A few devotions ago, I mentioned that some of those Persian records have been found by archaeologists and are available to this day. In other words, contrary to snarky, condescending internet atheists and Bible deniers, the Bible is a book of actual history, not a book of mythology!

When you read your Bible today, DO appreciate the fact that you are not just reading God's Word but also the most complete and accurate history book ever written!

Personal Notes:

_____

_____

_____

_____

_____

_____

_____

_____

_____

_____

_____

_____

_____

_____

_____

_____

_____

Devotion 14

The interference of the Samaritans caused trouble; more trouble than even they could have likely anticipated:

Ezra 4:21 *Give ye now commandment to cause these men to cease, and that this city be not builded, until another commandment shall be given from me.* **22** *Take heed now that ye fail not to do this: why should damage grow to the hurt of the kings?* **23** *Now when the copy of king Artaxerxes' letter was read before Rehum, and Shimshai the scribe, and their companions, they went up in haste to Jerusalem unto the Jews, and made them to cease by force and power.* **24** *Then ceased the work of the house of God which is at Jerusalem. So it ceased unto the second year of the reign of Darius king of Persia.*

There is a number you should remember here, the number fourteen. When verse twenty-four tells us that the work ceased until the second year of Darius, it means that for fourteen years, the temple construction was utterly stopped. But the second number you should know is five hundred and fifty. That is how many years passed before this exchange:

John 4:9 *Then saith the woman of Samaria unto him, How is it that thou, being a Jew, askest drink of me, which am a woman of Samaria? for the Jews have no dealings with the Samaritans.*

Five hundred fifty years. A needless spat, a group of people who could not stand that they were barred from what they wanted even though they could easily do what they wanted on their own land and on their own dime, caused nearly six centuries of animosity. That is doubtless more than they ever bargained for! And yet it is often the way things go with people.

Before you ever attack or pick a fight with someone, before you ever exchange harsh words, before you ever make that snarky comment online, DO ask yourself if you want your kids and grandkids and great-grandkids paying the price for it!

Personal Notes:

_____
_____
_____
_____
_____
_____
_____
_____
_____
_____
_____
_____
_____
_____
_____
_____
_____
_____
_____
_____
_____

Devotion 15

For fourteen years, the work on the house of God was stopped. Finally, though, two men who have books of the Bible named after them stepped up and got things moving again.

Ezra 5:1 *Then the prophets, Haggai the prophet, and Zechariah the son of Iddo, prophesied unto the Jews that were in Judah and Jerusalem in the name of the God of Israel, even unto them. **2** Then rose up Zerubbabel the son of Shealtiel, and Jeshua the son of Jozadak, and began to build the house of God which is at Jerusalem: and with them were the prophets of God helping them.*

If you read the books of Haggai and Zechariah, you will be reading what Ezra 5:1 says these two men prophesied to the people. In short, both of those men, but especially Haggai, preached scalding messages against the apathy of the people. In summary, their message went something like, "You have managed to build your own houses, you have looked out for your own well-being, and yet you do not give a rip about the ruin of the house of God. Stop making excuses and get back to work for God; fix the house of worship, faithfully attend it, and if you don't, you can expect God's judgment, not God's blessings."

How did the people respond? Verse two tells us that they rose up to build, and the two prophets joined in with them.

Excuses are easy; anyone can make them. But excuses never built a church, won a sinner to the Lord, or sent a missionary to the foreign field. DO dig into the house of God and the work of God, no excuses!

Personal Notes:

_____

_____

_____

_____

_____

_____

_____

_____

_____

_____

_____

_____

_____

_____

_____

_____

_____

_____

_____

_____

_____

_____

_____

_____

_____

_____

_____

_____

_____

_____

Devotion 16

Something quite remarkable takes place as we continue to examine the rebuilding of the temple and the opposition to it. After a fourteen-year delay, work started again at the urging of the prophets Haggai and Zechariah. Naturally, opposition popped up again. But it is the nature and tone of the opposition that is remarkable in this instance.

Ezra 5:3 *At the same time came to them Tatnai, governor on this side the river, and Shetharboznai, and their companions, and said thus unto them, Who hath commanded you to build this house, and to make up this wall?* **4** *Then said we unto them after this manner, What are the names of the men that make this building?* **5** *But the eye of their God was upon the elders of the Jews, that they could not cause them to cease, till the matter came to Darius: and then they returned answer by letter concerning this matter.*

It is clear that Tatnai and company were opposed to the rebuilding of the temple. And yet, everything that they said was actually moderate and careful, and the letter that they wrote to King Darius about the subject was fair, accurate, and non-emotional. When you finish this devotion, I encourage you to read the rest of Ezra 5 to see the text of that letter.

They were "opposed," but they were also fair and honorable.

What an example... and from people who likely were lost and without God, no less! How often do we, even when in the right, disagree in a manner that makes our right seem wrong!

DO make up your mind that, as much as is ever possible, you will be in the habit of disagreeing agreeably!

Personal Notes:

_____

_____

_____

_____

_____

_____

_____

_____

_____

_____

_____

_____

_____

_____

_____

_____

_____

_____

_____

_____

_____

_____

_____

_____

_____

Devotion 17

Tatnai and company sent a letter to Darius asking about the building of the House of God at Jerusalem, a project that they were opposed to. The records of Persia were searched, and here is what came out of that letter and search.

Ezra 6:1 *Then Darius the king made a decree, and search was made in the house of the rolls, where the treasures were laid up in Babylon.* **2** *And there was found at Achmetha, in the palace that is in the province of the Medes, a roll, and therein was a record thus written:* **3** *In the first year of Cyrus the king the same Cyrus the king made a decree concerning the house of God at Jerusalem, Let the house be builded, the place where they offered sacrifices, and let the foundations thereof be strongly laid; the height thereof threescore cubits, and the breadth thereof threescore cubits;* **4** *With three rows of great stones, and a row of new timber: and let the expenses be given out of the king's house:* **5** *And also let the golden and silver vessels of the house of God, which Nebuchadnezzar took forth out of the temple which is at Jerusalem, and brought unto Babylon, be restored, and brought again unto the temple which is at Jerusalem, every one to his place, and place them in the house of God.* **6** *Now therefore, Tatnai, governor beyond the river, Shetharboznai, and your companions the Apharsachites, which are beyond the river, be ye far from thence:* **7** *Let the work of this house of God alone; let the governor of the Jews and the elders of the Jews build this house of God in his place.*

Notice that statement, "Let the work of this house of God alone." We might say, "Back off; don't mess with them." How awesome is it that God, through Darius, sent such a letter, such backing for the work of the house of God!

God has always prized His house and the work that goes on there; if you were thinking of opposing it, DO back off and "let it alone!"

Personal Notes:

_____

_____

_____

_____

_____

_____

_____

_____

_____

_____

_____

_____

_____

_____

_____

_____

_____

_____

_____

_____

_____

_____

_____

Devotion 18

The amazing decree of Darius concerning the rebuilding of the house of God at Jerusalem just kept on getting better with each line:

Ezra 6:8 *Moreover I make a decree what ye shall do to the elders of these Jews for the building of this house of God: that of the king's goods, even of the tribute beyond the river, forthwith expenses be given unto these men, that they be not hindered. 9 And that which they have need of, both young bullocks, and rams, and lambs, for the burnt offerings of the God of heaven, wheat, salt, wine, and oil, according to the appointment of the priests which are at Jerusalem, let it be given them day by day without fail: 10 That they may offer sacrifices of sweet savours unto the God of heaven, and pray for the life of the king, and of his sons. 11 Also I have made a decree, that whosoever shall alter this word, let timber be pulled down from his house, and being set up, let him be hanged thereon; and let his house be made a dunghill for this. 12 And the God that hath caused his name to dwell there destroy all kings and people, that shall put to their hand to alter and to destroy this house of God which is at Jerusalem. I Darius have made a decree; let it be done with speed.*

In summary, Darius wrote, "Not only do I want you not to hinder the work, I expect you to write checks from the king's treasury to pay for it. I expect supplies from his flocks to be given for it, and if anyone opposes this, I will have his house pulled down, make gallows out of the wood, and hang him on it. Now snap to it!"

Wow! Why was Darius so intent on seeing this done? Perhaps because of a tiny phrase in verse ten, "and pray for the life of the king, and of his sons." Darius somehow knew that the Jews served a real and living God and that their prayers for him and his sons would make a difference.

DO be people of prayer; it will become known, and those you pray for will be inclined to advocate for you to men as you advocate for them to God!

Personal Notes:

_____
_____
_____
_____
_____
_____
_____
_____
_____
_____
_____
_____
_____
_____
_____
_____
_____
_____
_____
_____

Devotion 19

The adversaries of the temple being rebuilt had appealed to the king of Persia, and he had responded in unmistakable terms; the temple was to be rebuilt, and those adversaries were to facilitate the process. And that is exactly what quickly happened.

Ezra 6:13 *Then Tatnai, governor on this side the river, Shetharboznai, and their companions, according to that which Darius the king had sent, so they did speedily.* **14** *And the elders of the Jews builded, and they prospered through the prophesying of Haggai the prophet and Zechariah the son of Iddo. And they builded, and finished it, according to the commandment of the God of Israel, and according to the commandment of Cyrus, and Darius, and Artaxerxes king of Persia.* **15** *And this house was finished on the third day of the month Adar, which was in the sixth year of the reign of Darius the king.*

What is significant to me, among other things in these verses, is that three consecutive Persian kings threw their backing into the rebuilding of the temple of God. Cyrus, Darius, Artaxerxes; these were not what we would call "saved men!" They had their own "gods," their own beliefs, and their own theologies. They logically should have been the last people on earth to back this project. But when God chooses to do a work, He can use even His enemies to accomplish it!

We so often limit God in our thinking. We somehow believe that if the right people holding the right beliefs are available, God can do something great. But the truth is that even if all that is "available" are the wrong people holding the wrong beliefs, God is so much God that He can still do something great! Does He want people to be right and believe right? Yes. Is there any excuse for anyone to be wrong and believe wrong? No. But DO remember that God was all-powerful well before there was ever anyone to not believe right and do right, and He is still all-powerful now that there are!

Personal Notes:

_____

_____

_____

_____

_____

_____

_____

_____

_____

_____

_____

_____

_____

_____

_____

_____

_____

_____

_____

_____

Devotion 20

Against all odds, the temple of God was now rebuilt in Jerusalem. And, as at the building of the first Temple, there will be a dedication service. But the numbers given paint a rather vivid picture for us.

Ezra 6:16 *And the children of Israel, the priests, and the Levites, and the rest of the children of the captivity, kept the dedication of this house of God with joy,* **17** *And offered at the dedication of this house of God an hundred bullocks, two hundred rams, four hundred lambs; and for a sin offering for all Israel, twelve he goats, according to the number of the tribes of Israel.*

One hundred bullocks. Two hundred rams. Four hundred lambs. Now look back with me at the numbers given at the first dedication, the dedication of Solomon's Temple:

1 Kings 8:62 *And the king, and all Israel with him, offered sacrifice before the LORD.* **63** *And Solomon offered a sacrifice of peace offerings, which he offered unto the LORD, two and twenty thousand oxen, and an hundred and twenty thousand sheep. So the king and all the children of Israel dedicated the house of the LORD.*

Twenty-two thousand oxen. 120,000 sheep. Clearly, the children of Israel were remarkably less affluent at the building of the second Temple than they were at the building of the first. At the building of the first, they had a king; at the building of the second, all they had was a governor under tribute. It would be easy in a situation like that to compare the "glory of the past" with the "mediocrity of the present." But look at the reaction people had to the dedication of the smaller temple and the tiny offering compared to the past magnificent offering:

Ezra 6:21 *And the children of Israel, which were come again out of captivity, and all such as had separated themselves unto them from the filthiness of the heathen of the land, to seek the LORD God of Israel, did eat,* **22** *And kept the feast of unleavened bread seven days with joy: for the LORD had made them joyful, and turned the heart of the king of Assyria unto them, to strengthen their hands in the work of the house of God, the God of Israel.*

They were joyful. They had enough sense to appreciate what they presently had instead of begrudging what they had lost. And that is a wonderful formula for a joyful life.

Rather than focusing on what you once had or could have, DO be grateful for what you now have!

Personal Notes:

_____

_____

_____

_____

_____

_____

_____

_____

_____

_____

_____

Devotion 21

As chapter seven of the book of Ezra begins, many years have passed since the completion of the Temple in chapter six. And it is in chapter seven that Ezra himself, the figure for whom the book is named, comes into the account.

Ezra 7:1 *Now after these things, in the reign of Artaxerxes king of Persia, Ezra the son of Seraiah, the son of Azariah, the son of Hilkiah...*

Ezra 7:6 *This Ezra went up from Babylon; and he was a ready scribe in the law of Moses, which the LORD God of Israel had given: and the king granted him all his request, according to the hand of the LORD his God upon him.*

Ezra 7:10 *For Ezra had prepared his heart to seek the law of the LORD, and to do it, and to teach in Israel statutes and judgments.*

The temple had been rebuilt approximately sixty years earlier. And yet the temple, or church, if the people in it do not know how to conduct themselves, is nothing more than a storage building for ineffective saints. Ezra knew that this was playing out in Jerusalem. And so he determined to leave his post in Persia and travel to a land he had never been to so he could teach his people how to follow and obey God.

The most beautiful church building on earth will never really matter if God's people do not know how to conduct themselves when they get there. A Dunkin' Donuts can be beautiful, Chick-fil-A can be beautiful, a Hobby Lobby can be beautiful, and even the occasional Walmart can be beautiful. A church merely being beautiful means nothing until the behavior of the people within it is equally beautiful!

DO determine that the beauty of your behavior will match or exceed the beauty of your church surroundings!

Personal Notes:

_____

_____

_____

_____

_____

_____

_____

_____

_____

_____

_____

_____

_____

_____

_____

_____

_____

_____

_____

_____

_____

_____

_____

_____

Devotion 22

When Ezra came from Persia to Jerusalem, he came with a letter of decree from the king. And one particular thing in that letter is very important, even today.

Ezra 7:11 *Now this is the copy of the letter that the king Artaxerxes gave unto Ezra the priest, the scribe, even a scribe of the words of the commandments of the LORD, and of his statutes to Israel.* **12** *Artaxerxes, king of kings, unto Ezra the priest, a scribe of the law of the God of heaven, perfect peace, and at such a time.* **13** *I make a decree, that all they of the people of Israel, and of his priests and Levites, in my realm, which are minded of their own freewill to go up to Jerusalem, go with thee.* **14** *Forasmuch as thou art sent of the king, and of his seven counsellors, to enquire concerning Judah and Jerusalem, according to the law of thy God which is in thine hand;*

Ezra was sent specifically to teach his people how to obey God. In order to do that, they would have to know the law of God. And verse fourteen tells us that Ezra was carrying that very law in his hand.

This was the Scripture, the written Word of God. Even a pagan king understood that the Word of God was something that was written down, not something that was "felt in the heart." Our day is full of popular, nationally known preachers who constantly mock and minimize the importance of the written Word of God. They may couch their heresy in wonderful sounding phrases like, "All we need to know is that Jesus rose from the dead," or "The Holy Spirit will guide us," but the Jesus who rose from the dead repeatedly quoted Scripture as authoritative, and the Holy Spirit Himself was the author of Scripture!

If you want a "word from the Lord," DO take your left hand and right hand and open up your Bible. As soon as you do, you have a Word from the Lord!

Personal Notes:

_____

_____

_____

_____

_____

_____

_____

_____

_____

_____

_____

_____

_____

_____

_____

_____

_____

_____

_____

_____

_____

_____

Devotion 23

As the decree of the king to Ezra continued on, it got to the point of money.

Ezra 7:15 *And to carry the silver and gold, which the king and his counsellors have freely offered unto the God of Israel, whose habitation is in Jerusalem,* **16** *And all the silver and gold that thou canst find in all the province of Babylon, with the freewill offering of the people, and of the priests, offering willingly for the house of their God which is in Jerusalem:* **17** *That thou mayest buy speedily with this money bullocks, rams, lambs, with their meat offerings and their drink offerings, and offer them upon the altar of the house of your God which is in Jerusalem.* **18** *And whatsoever shall seem good to thee, and to thy brethren, to do with the rest of the silver and the gold, that do after the will of your God.*

Throughout the Bible, those who worshipped God did so not just with their hands and heart and mouth but also with their treasures, their money. A person can shout louder than a college cheerleader, jump higher than a pole vaulter, and sing like the angels of glory, but if their "worship" never reaches their wallet, it isn't real worship!

In any church, you will find takers (people who simply consume without ever giving anything at all), tippers (people who occasionally "bless the Lord's heart" by dropping a wrinkled-up dollar bill or two into the offering plate), and tithers (people who truly worship the Lord with their substance.)

DO be a true worshipper; be a tither!

Personal Notes:

_____
_____
_____
_____
_____
_____
_____
_____
_____
_____
_____
_____
_____
_____
_____
_____
_____
_____
_____
_____
_____
_____
_____
_____
_____
_____
_____
_____
_____
_____
_____
_____

Devotion 24

As the decree of the king to Ezra continued to unfold, it even reached the point of discussing "the church and taxes."

Ezra 7:21 *And I, even I Artaxerxes the king, do make a decree to all the treasurers which are beyond the river, that whatsoever Ezra the priest, the scribe of the law of the God of heaven, shall require of you, it be done speedily,* **22** *Unto an hundred talents of silver, and to an hundred measures of wheat, and to an hundred baths of wine, and to an hundred baths of oil, and salt without prescribing how much.* **23** *Whatsoever is commanded by the God of heaven, let it be diligently done for the house of the God of heaven: for why should there be wrath against the realm of the king and his sons?* **24** *Also we certify you, that touching any of the priests and Levites, singers, porters, Nethinims, or ministers of this house of God, it shall not be lawful to impose toll, tribute, or custom, upon them.*

Toll, tribute, and custom were three words for taxes. The concept of a ministry being tax-free is a very old concept, not at all a new concept! Simply put, wise governments throughout the ages have understood that a body of believers meeting together for worship is such a valuable thing for society that it should not be taxed. Not taxing ministries encourages ministries to exist and thrive.

When your leftist friends make snarky comments about it being time to tax churches, DO remind them that they have been on the wrong side of history on that one for thousands of years already!

Personal Notes:

_____
_____
_____
_____
_____
_____
_____
_____
_____
_____
_____
_____
_____
_____
_____
_____
_____
_____
_____
_____
_____
_____
_____
_____
_____
_____
_____
_____

Devotion 25

As the king's letter to Ezra came to an end, we see more of the amazing grace and provision of God.

Ezra 7:25 *And thou, Ezra, after the wisdom of thy God, that is in thine hand, set magistrates and judges, which may judge all the people that are beyond the river, all such as know the laws of thy God; and teach ye them that know them not. 26 And whosoever will not do the law of thy God, and the law of the king, let judgment be executed speedily upon him, whether it be unto death, or to banishment, or to confiscation of goods, or to imprisonment. 27 Blessed be the LORD God of our fathers, which hath put such a thing as this in the king's heart, to beautify the house of the LORD which is in Jerusalem: 28 And hath extended mercy unto me before the king, and his counsellors, and before all the king's mighty princes. And I was strengthened as the hand of the LORD my God was upon me, and I gathered together out of Israel chief men to go up with me.*

In verse fourteen, the king mentioned the law of God that was physically in Ezra's hand. Now here in verse twenty-five, he references the Scripture again, calling it the wisdom of God that is *"in thine hand."* This was a pagan king recognizing the authority of Scripture. Little wonder, then, that Ezra said, "Blessed be the LORD God of our fathers, which hath put such a thing as this in the king's heart, to beautify the house of the LORD which is in Jerusalem." He recognized that every bit of this was the God of heaven moving the heart of the least likely person, a Persian monarch, to behave in such a manner.

Throughout history, God has moved the hearts of dictators and tyrants and kings and presidents in such a way that His people come out blessed for it. We so often get hopeless at the world around us and think, "What's the use? The fix is already in!" You will hear that nearly every election cycle from people who believe that powerful unseen forces already make all of the decisions.

But while they may want to, and while they may try to, there is no conspiracy or cabal more powerful than the God on the throne. So DO continue to move forward in the assurance that God has the last say in everything!

Personal Notes:

_____

_____

_____

_____

_____

_____

_____

_____

_____

_____

_____

_____

_____

_____

_____

Devotion 26

When Ezra made his way from Persia to Jerusalem, the numbers given in chapter eight tell us that 1,754 adult men made their way there with him, which would make for a caravan of 6,000 to 7,000 when women and children are included. But as he examined who was coming, he quickly realized he had a problem.

Ezra 8:15 *And I gathered them together to the river that runneth to Ahava; and there abode we in tents three days: and I viewed the people, and the priests, and found there none of the sons of Levi.*

In the service of the Lord's house, there were the priests, who were of the tribe of Levi, and then there were the other men of the tribe of Levi who were not priests but who were supposed to be assisting in the service of the Lord's house. If we were to put it in a church context, we would say, "There were preachers in the caravan, but no ministering laymen."

And God has never expected it to be that way. He has always expected both His men in the pulpit and His people in the pews to be engaged in the service of God together. There will simply always be too much to do for a small handful to pull the cart while everyone else rides in the back.

In any effective church, there will not just be a good preacher in the pulpit, but also singers and nursery workers and ushers and security and sound men and musicians and custodians and ushers and deacons and a thousand other tasks that make the work of the church run smoothly. So DO always be in your place, and DO always be pulling your weight!

Personal Notes:

_____

_____

_____

_____

_____

_____

_____

_____

_____

_____

_____

_____

_____

_____

_____

_____

_____

_____

_____

_____

_____

_____

_____

_____

_____

_____

_____

Devotion 27

When Ezra realized that they were shorthanded, having no Levites for the service of the Lord's house, he sent word to a man named Iddo, asking for the help they needed.

Ezra 8:16 *Then sent I for Eliezer, for Ariel, for Shemaiah, and for Elnathan, and for Jarib, and for Elnathan, and for Nathan, and for Zechariah, and for Meshullam, chief men; also for Joiarib, and for Elnathan, men of understanding.* **17** *And I sent them with commandment unto Iddo the chief at the place Casiphia, and I told them what they should say unto Iddo, and to his brethren the Nethinims, at the place Casiphia, that they should bring unto us ministers for the house of our God.* **18** *And by the good hand of our God upon us they brought us a man of understanding, of the sons of Mahli, the son of Levi, the son of Israel; and Sherebiah, with his sons and his brethren, eighteen;* **19** *And Hashabiah, and with him Jeshaiah of the sons of Merari, his brethren and their sons, twenty;* **20** *Also of the Nethinims, whom David and the princes had appointed for the service of the Levites, two hundred and twenty Nethinims: all of them were expressed by name.*

The general call had not been enough, and that is truly a shame. But this specific call, naming names, finally got some of the Levites headed in the right direction into the service of the Lord. But the brightest of the bright spots in all of this is that two hundred twenty Nethinims answered the call, far more than any other group of the Levites.

Who in the world were the Nethinims?

The Nethinims were mostly temple servants and originally were of foreign origin. They performed the lowest and most menial tasks in the temple. They were sort of "the assistant custodians to the custodians of the custodians." And yet these anonymous nobodies stepped up to the task far more fully than any of the "people of pedigree."

But if you were trying to do a work for God, who would you rather have, the "snoots" or the servants?

DO be willing to do the most unwanted and unnoticed of tasks because God Himself wants them done and notices when they are!

Personal Notes:

_____

_____

_____

_____

_____

_____

_____

_____

_____

_____

_____

_____

_____

_____

_____

_____

Devotion 28

Having gotten all of the ministers together for the service of the house of the Lord, Ezra did one more thing before they started on their journey back toward Jerusalem, and truthfully, it is both an instructive thing and a bit of a funny thing.

Ezra 8:21 *Then I proclaimed a fast there, at the river of Ahava, that we might afflict ourselves before our God, to seek of him a right way for us, and for our little ones, and for all our substance.* **22** *For I was ashamed to require of the king a band of soldiers and horsemen to help us against the enemy in the way: because we had spoken unto the king, saying, The hand of our God is upon all them for good that seek him; but his power and his wrath is against all them that forsake him.* **23** *So we fasted and besought our God for this: and he was intreated of us.*

Ezra was getting ready to march across hostile terrain into a broken-down city surrounded by enemies. He was allowed to do so because he had convinced the king that his God was real and all-powerful and wanted to have proper worship established in Jerusalem. But that caused a bit of a conundrum; how could Ezra paint God in that light to the king and then say, "Now, could you send some soldiers to protect us along the way?" He knew exactly how that would look.

This was a very good case of living what you say you believe. Ezra had everyone fast and pray, and then they took their journey without human protection, being willing to risk their lives rather than risking sending a mixed message.

To be clear, there is nothing wrong with human protection or with things like guns or insurance to accomplish it. I recommend both. But there is something wrong with telling the lost world that your God will take care of you and then asking the lost world to take care of you "in case He doesn't" because you were too lazy or proud to do your part! This is more common than you might think, especially among people who piously refuse to get insurance because "That would show a lack of faith" and then start a GoFundMe page as soon as something goes wrong.

DO be consistent with what you believe, especially before the lost world who is watching everything you do and say!

Personal Notes:

_____
_____
_____
_____
_____
_____
_____
_____
_____
_____
_____
_____
_____
_____

Devotion 29

Please notice a matter of incredibly practical wisdom that Ezra demonstrated as they began their journey back to Jerusalem.

Ezra 8:24 *Then I separated twelve of the chief of the priests, Sherebiah, Hashabiah, and ten of their brethren with them,* **25** *And weighed unto them the silver, and the gold, and the vessels, even the offering of the house of our God, which the king, and his counsellors, and his lords, and all Israel there present, had offered:* **26** *I even weighed unto their hand six hundred and fifty talents of silver, and silver vessels an hundred talents, and of gold an hundred talents;* **27** *Also twenty basons of gold, of a thousand drams; and two vessels of fine copper, precious as gold.* **28** *And I said unto them, Ye are holy unto the LORD; the vessels are holy also; and the silver and the gold are a freewill offering unto the LORD God of your fathers.* **29** *Watch ye, and keep them, until ye weigh them before the chief of the priests and the Levites, and chief of the fathers of Israel, at Jerusalem, in the chambers of the house of the LORD.*

They were making their way across hostile territory with an incredible amount of wealth. And Ezra, using very practical wisdom, separated that wealth between twenty-four different men* and told them to watch it and keep it. That way, if anyone was attacked, the others could scatter and escape with what they had. Today we call that "diversification." The old-timers would have called it "Not putting all of your eggs in one basket."

It is amazing how much practical wisdom is to be found in God's Word!

DO understand the power of diversification, and DO put it into practice, especially in financial matters!

*Twelve priests, two Levites (Sherebiah and Hashabiah), and ten more Levites with Sherebiah and Hashabiah.

Personal Notes:

_____

_____

_____

_____

_____

_____

_____

_____

_____

_____

_____

_____

_____

_____

_____

_____

_____

_____

_____

_____

_____

_____

_____

Devotion 30

Once everything was in place and the wealth distributed between several people, Ezra and his company made their way to Jerusalem.

Ezra 8:31 *Then we departed from the river of Ahava on the twelfth day of the first month, to go unto Jerusalem: and the hand of our God was upon us, and he delivered us from the hand of the enemy, and of such as lay in wait by the way.* **32** *And we came to Jerusalem, and abode there three days.*

Comparing this passage with Ezra 7:9, we find that the journey from Persia to Jerusalem took them three- and one-half months. And it was not an easy journey. God had to deliver them from the hands of enemies and from people who were lying in wait for them along the way. And that is why what we read in verse thirty-two makes such perfect sense. When they arrived in Jerusalem, they did not immediately start to work; they rested for three days before they did anything.

In the very beginning, the God who never needs any rest established a pattern for mankind, resting Himself after working for six days at creating the universe. God intends for His people to have a good balance between work and rest. Especially after some huge lengthy task, it is good to take an extended period of rest. God gave us exactly one body and exactly one life; ruining that body and shortening that life by refusing to ever rest is neither wise nor honorable.

DO get some rest!

Personal Notes:

Devotion 31

Once the travelers had rested for three days, they got to work on the task at hand.

Ezra 8:33 *Now on the fourth day was the silver and the gold and the vessels weighed in the house of our God by the hand of Meremoth the son of Uriah the priest; and with him was Eleazar the son of Phinehas; and with them was Jozabad the son of Jeshua, and Noadiah the son of Binnui, Levites;* **34** *By number and by weight of every one: and all the weight was written at that time.* **35** *Also the children of those that had been carried away, which were come out of the captivity, offered burnt offerings unto the God of Israel, twelve bullocks for all Israel, ninety and six rams, seventy and seven lambs, twelve he goats for a sin offering: all this was a burnt offering unto the LORD.* **36** *And they delivered the king's commissions unto the king's lieutenants, and to the governors on this side the river: and they furthered the people, and the house of God.*

In these verses, we find that the people who had been entrusted with the care of the silver and gold had been faithful and careful in their tasks. But we also find something else very encouraging at the end of verse thirty-six. They, meaning the people who were in charge around them, who had previously been opposed to them and what they were doing, "furthered" both the people of God and the house of God. They got behind what was going on and helped. Those who had been, in our vernacular, "anti-Christian and anti-Church" at the command of the king became a help to both.

God is very good at bringing help from the least likely sources! But the main thing on my heart at this point is this question: are WE furthering the people of God and the house of God? It is one thing to rejoice that God helps His work and His people by putting pressure on the lost world to do so; it is quite another to step up to the plate and help His work and His people just because we are His people in His work and have a heart for what is going on.

DO "further" the work of God and the people of God by your efforts!

Personal Notes:

_____

_____

_____

_____

_____

_____

_____

_____

_____

_____

_____

_____

_____

_____

_____

_____

_____

_____

_____

_____

Devotion 32

Everything seemed to be going so well in the quest to reestablish proper worship in the recently rebuilt house of God in Jerusalem. But the devil is never idle, especially not when the work of God is moving forward. And suddenly, the awareness of a huge problem cropped up.

Ezra 9:1 *Now when these things were done, the princes came to me, saying, The people of Israel, and the priests, and the Levites, have not separated themselves from the people of the lands, doing according to their abominations, even of the Canaanites, the Hittites, the Perizzites, the Jebusites, the Ammonites, the Moabites, the Egyptians, and the Amorites. 2 For they have taken of their daughters for themselves, and for their sons: so that the holy seed have mingled themselves with the people of those lands: yea, the hand of the princes and rulers hath been chief in this trespass. 3 And when I heard this thing, I rent my garment and my mantle, and plucked off the hair of my head and of my beard, and sat down astonied.*

The people of Israel, and, sadly, especially their leaders, the ones they should have been able to look to for a godly example of behavior, had been intermarrying with the wicked heathens around them and following those heathens into their filthy idol worship. And this problem was not recent; it had clearly been going on since well before Ezra arrived. And it was a direct violation of the specific law of God given by His mouth to Moses. This was not some small thing, new thing, or surprising thing.

When Ezra heard all of this, he was so stunned that he literally pulled handfuls of his own hair and beard out. When you have "made the preacher pull his hair out," it probably isn't a good thing.

Are you a Christian, a true follower of Christ? Then DO have proper separation in your life; we are never to mix and mingle with the lost world in marriage or morals!

Personal Notes:

_____

_____

_____

_____

_____

_____

_____

_____

_____

_____

_____

_____

_____

_____

_____

_____

_____

_____

_____

_____

_____

Devotion 33

Ezra had physically pulled hair off his head and beard off of his face when he realized the horrible things the children of Israel, especially their leaders, had done in marrying the heathens around them and following their gods. Here is what came next in that heartbreaking episode.

Ezra 9:4 *Then were assembled unto me every one that trembled at the words of the God of Israel, because of the transgression of those that had been carried away; and I sat astonied until the evening sacrifice. 5 And at the evening sacrifice I arose up from my heaviness; and having rent my garment and my mantle, I fell upon my knees, and spread out my hands unto the LORD my God, 6 And said, O my God, I am ashamed and blush to lift up my face to thee, my God: for our iniquities are increased over our head, and our trespass is grown up unto the heavens.*

There is in this response of Ezra to the sin of the people a good picture of what our attitude ought to be toward sin. In their day, like in ours, people viewed "acts between consenting adults" as something that was none of God's business. But in their day, like it should be in ours, Ezra and true believers around him said that they were ashamed and blushing to even lift up their faces to God. They openly proclaimed, "Our iniquities are increased over our head, and our trespass is grown up under the heavens."

That is exactly how we ought to feel about sin.

For years, many mainline churches have simply shrugged off things like adultery and premarital sex and fornication, and now two consecutive presidents of the Southern Baptist Convention have opined that "the Bible only whispers about homosexuality." We are right back in the days of Ezra, where anything goes, and none of it is any of God's business.

But it is God's business. All of it. And when a people is not just sinful but proud of their sinfulness, they are very near to destruction. Our proper response to any sinfulness should be embarrassment, not pride.

When it comes to sin, DO use this statement over and over again, "It IS God's business!"

Personal Notes:

_____

_____

_____

_____

_____

_____

_____

_____

_____

_____

_____

_____

_____

_____

_____

_____

_____

_____

Devotion 34

In his prayer, Ezra spoke passionately about the shame and embarrassment he felt over the sin of his people. But then he segued into a bit of a history lesson that showed how well he understood the situation at hand and the trouble they were in.

Ezra 9:7 *Since the days of our fathers have we been in a great trespass unto this day; and for our iniquities have we, our kings, and our priests, been delivered into the hand of the kings of the lands, to the sword, to captivity, and to a spoil, and to confusion of face, as it is this day.* **8** *And now for a little space grace hath been shewed from the LORD our God, to leave us a remnant to escape, and to give us a nail in his holy place, that our God may lighten our eyes, and give us a little reviving in our bondage.* **9** *For we were bondmen; yet our God hath not forsaken us in our bondage, but hath extended mercy unto us in the sight of the kings of Persia, to give us a reviving, to set up the house of our God, and to repair the desolations thereof, and to give us a wall in Judah and in Jerusalem.*

In those few short words, Ezra summarized nearly a thousand years of Jewish history. From the very first generation of them that God brought out of Egypt, it had been rebellion after rebellion after rebellion against God. Because of that, God had once and again allowed them to fall captive to enemy nations. They had just come through their most brutal captivity since Egypt itself, seventy years in Babylon. The Babylonian captivity had given way to exile in

Persia. And now God had extended mercy to them in the sight of the kings of Persia.

There is one phrase in verse eight that is really picturesque. Ezra said that God had been gracious to *"give us a nail in his holy place."* He was talking about a tent peg. It was a euphemism for driving a stake and setting up a tent if you intended to stay somewhere for a while. It was nothing glorious like a house or palace, but after nearly one hundred years of upheaval, even being allowed to drive a nail into the ground for your tent was an undeserved paradise on earth.

Most people would not have been so impressed with a simple tent peg. And that is because most people did not have the grasp of history that Ezra had. When we realize where God has brought us from and just how little we deserve, we will be infinitely grateful for even the small things!

So I have a suggestion for you. DO find yourself a nail, put it somewhere that you will see it regularly, and allow it to remind you of just how good God has been!

Personal Notes:

_____

_____

_____

_____

_____

_____

_____

_____

_____

Devotion 35

Ezra was still pouring out his heart in anguish to God over the people and the leaders joining in wicked marriages and wicked morals with the people of the lands around them:

Ezra 9:10 *And now, O our God, what shall we say after this? for we have forsaken thy commandments,* **11** *Which thou hast commanded by thy servants the prophets, saying, The land, unto which ye go to possess it, is an unclean land with the filthiness of the people of the lands, with their abominations, which have filled it from one end to another with their uncleanness.* **12** *Now therefore give not your daughters unto their sons, neither take their daughters unto your sons, nor seek their peace or their wealth for ever: that ye may be strong, and eat the good of the land, and leave it for an inheritance to your children for ever.* **13** *And after all that is come upon us for our evil deeds, and for our great trespass, seeing that thou our God hast punished us less than our iniquities deserve, and hast given us such deliverance as this;* **14** *Should we again break thy commandments, and join in affinity with the people of these abominations? wouldest not thou be angry with us till thou hadst consumed us, so that there should be no remnant nor escaping?* **15** *O LORD God of Israel, thou art righteous: for we remain yet escaped, as it is this day: behold, we are before thee in our trespasses: for we cannot stand before thee because of this.*

God was angry over His people intermarrying with other people around them. But He had a very good reason to not want them to do so, and we begin to find it in the words "Now therefore" in verse twelve. And the "therefore" that God had, had nothing at all to do with skin and everything to do with sin! It was, in His words, about their filthiness, uncleanness, and abominations. Simply put, as 2 Corinthians 6:14 makes clear, even in the New Testament era, our era, it is never acceptable for a believer to marry a non-believer.

You who are single, DO vow before God that you will never marry a non-believer, and you who are raising kids and grandkids, DO teach them that principle early and often!

Personal Notes:

_____

_____

_____

_____

_____

_____

_____

_____

_____

_____

_____

_____

_____

_____

_____

_____

_____

Devotion 36

Ezra had wept and prayed before God over the terrible sin of the people. It seemed there was no way to avoid the disaster of judgment, and he was brokenhearted both over the sin and over the consequences to come. But as chapter ten begins, we see a tiny ray of light break through the dark clouds.

Ezra 10:1 *Now when Ezra had prayed, and when he had confessed, weeping and casting himself down before the house of God, there assembled unto him out of Israel a very great congregation of men and women and children: for the people wept very sore.* **2** *And Shechaniah the son of Jehiel, one of the sons of Elam, answered and said unto Ezra, We have trespassed against our God, and have taken strange wives of the people of the land: yet now there is hope in Israel concerning this thing.*

In response to Ezra's repentance and prayer for his people, the people themselves, a huge multitude of them, gathered themselves to him to see if things could be made right. And one man, Shechaniah, determined that they could. In verse two, he said, *"Yet now there is hope in Israel concerning this thing."*

There is hope. We will begin in the next devotion to look at what that hope entailed, but for now, just understand one very important thing: no matter how badly people have sinned and made a mess of their lives, if they truly want to get right with God, there is always hope.

Have you made a mess of things in your life? DO be assured that there is still hope!

Personal Notes:

_____
_____
_____
_____
_____
_____
_____
_____
_____
_____
_____
_____
_____
_____
_____
_____
_____
_____
_____
_____
_____
_____
_____
_____
_____
_____
_____
_____
_____
_____

Devotion 37

In response to the weeping and mourning and prayer of Ezra over the horrendous sin of the people, Shecaniah acknowledged the trespass but then said, "There is still hope." And as I said in the last devotion, when people are willing to repent and get right with God, there is always hope. But now we need to flip the coin over and see the other side because that "hope" came at a steep cost.

Ezra 10:3 *Now therefore let us make a covenant with our God to put away all the wives, and such as are born of them, according to the counsel of my lord, and of those that tremble at the commandment of our God; and let it be done according to the law. 4 Arise; for this matter belongeth unto thee: we also will be with thee: be of good courage, and do it.*

Israelite men had married heathen women from the idolatrous nations around them and followed them into that idolatry, and some had even produced children by that point. All of that was clearly and utterly forbidden under the Mosaic law. The solution that Shecaniah recommended to Ezra was that they divorce those wives and remove both wives and children from the home.

In the New Testament era, we are given a very different command when a believer has somehow married an unbeliever. **1 Corinthians 7:12-13** says, "*But to the rest speak I, not the Lord: If any brother hath a wife that believeth not, and she be pleased to dwell with him, let him not put her away. And the* *woman which hath an husband that believeth not, and if he be pleased to dwell with her, let her not leave him.*" But the fact that the "solution" to the problem is different now is not what I want to focus on at this point. What I want everyone to understand from what you see in Ezra 10 is that sin often leaves us with no truly good options, only "less bad" options. Allowing idolatry to flourish in the land because of those wrong marriages was a horrible option. Having to bust up homes to fix the problem was an only slightly less horrible option, even though the wives and children were almost assuredly financially cared for.

The point is, if you really want to have a good option when dealing with sin, you will usually only find it before the sin, not after the sin. So DO leave yourself the only perfect option when dealing with sin; DO refrain from sin to begin with!

Personal Notes:

_____
_____
_____
_____
_____
_____
_____
_____
_____
_____
_____
_____
_____

Devotion 38

The plan of action to fix the problem created by the sin of the people had been decided upon. The next step would be to summon everyone and let them know how things were going to be from that moment forward.

Ezra 10:5 *Then arose Ezra, and made the chief priests, the Levites, and all Israel, to swear that they should do according to this word. And they sware.* **6** *Then Ezra rose up from before the house of God, and went into the chamber of Johanan the son of Eliashib: and when he came thither, he did eat no bread, nor drink water: for he mourned because of the transgression of them that had been carried away.* **7** *And they made proclamation throughout Judah and Jerusalem unto all the children of the captivity, that they should gather themselves together unto Jerusalem;* **8** *And that whosoever would not come within three days, according to the counsel of the princes and the elders, all his substance should be forfeited, and himself separated from the congregation of those that had been carried away.*

It is almost a bit funny to look at the teeth that Ezra and the leadership of Israel put into their summons. Knowing how badly everyone needed to hear the message, they passed a law and put it into the proclamation that whoever did not come to Jerusalem to hear the decision of the princes and elders on this matter would have everything they owned taken away from them and be excommunicated from the congregation.

That is a really good way to avoid any, "Well, if I don't have any other pressing matters, I'll do my best to make it." It is also a good testimony to how lackadaisical people normally are concerning the things of God. Why should any pressure at all have to ever be exerted to get people to meet and hear from the Lord? Especially in this era of grace where Christ willingly gave all for us, and we have His precious, completed Word, it should never take any kind of pressure to get us to show up and hear His Word.

DO be faithful; DO keep a pastor from ever mumbling, "Maybe things weren't so bad the way they did them in the Old Testament!"

Personal Notes:

_____

_____

_____

_____

_____

_____

_____

_____

_____

_____

_____

_____

_____

_____

_____

_____

_____

_____

Devotion 39

Quick! Finish this common phrase, "When it rains, it _____."

With that truism in mind, let's go back to Ezra and find out how things went with the summons for everyone to come to hear the judgment of the elders and princes.

Ezra 10:9 *Then all the men of Judah and Benjamin gathered themselves together unto Jerusalem within three days. It was the ninth month, on the twentieth day of the month; and all the people sat in the street of the house of God, trembling because of this matter, and for the great rain.* **10** *And Ezra the priest stood up, and said unto them, Ye have transgressed, and have taken strange wives, to increase the trespass of Israel.* **11** *Now therefore make confession unto the LORD God of your fathers, and do his pleasure: and separate yourselves from the people of the land, and from the strange wives.* **12** *Then all the congregation answered and said with a loud voice, As thou hast said, so must we do.* **13** *But the people are many, and it is a time of much rain, and we are not able to stand without, neither is this a work of one day or two: for we are many that have transgressed in this thing.* **14** *Let now our rulers of all the congregation stand, and let all them which have taken strange wives in our cities come at appointed times, and with them the elders of every city, and the judges thereof, until the fierce wrath of our God for this matter be turned from us.*

I seriously think that God has a great sense of humor even when wrathful. Everyone arrives for their lecture, and as if that isn't going to be bad enough, God sends an absolute downpour on all of them. Ezra, for his part, calmly stands up and preaches to them, demanding that they repent and make things right. Their answer can be paraphrased as follows: "Okay, Preacher, you're right; you got us. We will do everything you say. But it's going to take a little while to actually do it, and it will need to be organized, so can we please come in out of the rain now?"

When the circumstances of life make us say, "When it rains, it pours," that is bad enough. But when our sin has brought us to the place where we are being scalded by a preacher while standing in the driving rain for his message, that is hysterically awful!

DO make sure that all of your "when it rains, it pours" moments are caused by circumstances, not by sin!

Personal Notes:

_____
_____
_____
_____
_____
_____
_____
_____
_____
_____
_____

Devotion 40

The decision was made, everyone had agreed, and when they finally got dried out, they set about fulfilling the promise. Here is how that went and how long it took.

Ezra 10:15 *Only Jonathan the son of Asahel and Jahaziah the son of Tikvah were employed about this matter: and Meshullam and Shabbethai the Levite helped them.* **16** *And the children of the captivity did so. And Ezra the priest, with certain chief of the fathers, after the house of their fathers, and all of them by their names, were separated, and sat down in the first day of the tenth month to examine the matter.* **17** *And they made an end with all the men that had taken strange wives by the first day of the first month.*

There were two men in charge of handling all of the divorces and two other men helping them. And the entire process took from the first day of the tenth month to the first day of the first month, three whole months. For three whole months, Jonathan and Jahaziah spent all day every day saying something like, "I now un-pronounce you man and wife." If we were to put this scene in the modern day, we would say for three months, jewelers were overwhelmed with the return of wedding rings, photographers knew the people were not even going to bother to show up to pick up their pictures, and florists were going to be saying, "Too late, Jack; those flowers are already dead!"

What a disaster! But isn't that to be expected when we simply ignore God's Word and do things our own way?

DO be wise enough to always do things God's way from the very outset; things done wrong easily are rarely set right easily!

Personal Notes:

_____

_____

_____

_____

_____

_____

_____

_____

_____

_____

_____

_____

_____

_____

_____

_____

_____

_____

_____

_____

_____

_____

Devotion 41

As the book of Ezra draws to a close, we reach what was for the men involved in their great sin a "gulp!" moment.

Ezra 10:18 *And among the sons of the priests there were found that had taken strange wives: namely, of the sons of Jeshua the son of Jozadak, and his brethren; Maaseiah, and Eliezer, and Jarib, and Gedaliah.* **19** *And they gave their hands that they would put away their wives; and being guilty, they offered a ram of the flock for their trespass.*

Many years ago, the incomparable Ray Stevens wrote a song called "The Mississippi Squirrel Revival." One of the funniest lines in that song is, "And then she started naming names!" But 2,500 years or so before there ever was a "Sister Bertha Better Than You," there was "The Return from Captivity Revival," and the person naming names was Ezra. We have thus far been dealing with the general truth that "some people" had married idolatrous heathen wives. But from verse eighteen until the end of the chapter, we are given 114 names of important people who were guilty of this grievous sin. It is 2,500 years later, and we are still reading their names.

This should give us some sense of how seriously God expects us to take holiness. If He was willing to name names and write them down and record them in His precious Word for all eternity, then He is very, very serious about us living lives of holiness!

Do you hate being embarrassed? Then DO make sure you never give God a good reason to "take names and kick patooties!"

Personal Notes:

_____

_____

_____

_____

_____

_____

_____

_____

_____

_____

_____

_____

_____

_____

_____

_____

_____

_____

_____

_____

_____

_____

_____

_____

Devotion 42

We now arrive in the book of Nehemiah. To put it in chronological context, Ezra led his return in 458 BC, and the events of the book of Nehemiah began fourteen years later in 444 BC. And while Ezra had been concerned with the deeply spiritual matter of reestablishing proper temple worship, Nehemiah was concerned with a far more practical matter.

Nehemiah 1:1 *The words of Nehemiah the son of Hachaliah. And it came to pass in the month Chisleu, in the twentieth year, as I was in Shushan the palace,* **2** *That Hanani, one of my brethren, came, he and certain men of Judah; and I asked them concerning the Jews that had escaped, which were left of the captivity, and concerning Jerusalem.* **3** *And they said unto me, The remnant that are left of the captivity there in the province are in great affliction and reproach: the wall of Jerusalem also is broken down, and the gates thereof are burned with fire.* **4** *And it came to pass, when I heard these words, that I sat down and wept, and mourned certain days, and fasted, and prayed before the God of heaven,*

All of the events of Nehemiah are centered around the rebuilding of the walls and gates of the city of Jerusalem. Nehemiah heard a firsthand account that the walls were broken down, and his response was to weep and mourn and fast and pray.

Let that sink in; he responded to practical matters among God's people the way that Ezra responded to spiritual matters around God's people. God put two books in the Bible back-to-back, two heroes in the Bible back-to-back, and two perspectives in the Bible back-to-back to let us know that we should have a heavy burden both for all things spiritual and all things practical in the things of God. We should have a burden for soul-winning and for church carpet cleaning, missions and building projects, prayer and good sound systems, the Lord's supper and a nice church kitchen. The spiritual without the practical will be nothing but a lofty dream, and the practical without the spiritual will be nothing but a hollow edifice.

DO be burdened for both the spiritual and the practical!

Personal Notes:

_____

_____

_____

_____

_____

_____

_____

_____

_____

_____

_____

_____

_____

_____

_____

_____

_____

_____

Devotion 43

As Nehemiah began to pray, he began at a place where it is always good to begin our prayers, with the recognition of the character of God.

Nehemiah 1:5 *And said, I beseech thee, O LORD God of heaven, the great and terrible God, that keepeth covenant and mercy for them that love him and observe his commandments:*

Nehemiah called God "great and terrible." When we think of terrible, we are thinking usually in negative terms. But the biblical word for terrible comes from the word "terror," and it means that God is so great and so powerful that anyone in their right mind would fear before Him. You may think that is a dark and dreary view of God. But not when you are on His side! When you are on His side and your enemies are bigger than you, it is good to know that He is bigger than your enemies!

But Nehemiah went on in verse five to view the softer side of God as well, the fact that God will keep His promises and show mercy toward those who obey Him. In other words, God is not looking for a reason to destroy us; He is looking for a reason to bless us!

DO rejoice both in the fact that God is terrible and in the fact that He is merciful; both of those things should be a joy to anyone who truly lives for God!

Personal Notes:

Devotion 44

As Nehemiah continued his brokenhearted prayer, we are made privy to the length and breadth of those prayers:

Nehemiah 1:6 *Let thine ear now be attentive, and thine eyes open, that thou mayest hear the prayer of thy servant, which I pray before thee now, day and night, for the children of Israel thy servants, and confess the sins of the children of Israel, which we have sinned against thee: both I and my father's house have sinned.*

As to the length of those prayers, Nehemiah was praying both day and night; this is an indication that he was praying without ceasing over the matter. As to the breadth of those prayers, Nehemiah encompassed himself in with the children of Israel, saying, *"Both I and my father's house have sinned."* So Nehemiah's prayers were both constant and contemplative. He was praying all the time, and he had enough spiritual discernment to include himself in the list of those who needed the mercy of God in this matter.

And that is exactly how long and broad our own prayer life should be. Our prayer lives, which I surmise take up probably the smallest portion of our day, need to become prayer lives that are active throughout the day. And rather than looking at "those sinners out there in the world" as we pray, we need to consistently take stock of the fact that we are every much as in need of the mercy of God as everyone else.

DO have a prayer life with the length and breadth of that of Nehemiah!

Personal Notes:

_____

_____

_____

_____

_____

_____

_____

_____

_____

_____

_____

_____

_____

_____

_____

_____

_____

_____

_____

_____

_____

_____

_____

_____

_____

_____

_____

_____

Devotion 45

Nehemiah continued to pour out his prayer to God. But as he got to the end of it, he made a seemingly innocuous comment that, in reality, was anything but. In fact, it is utterly earth-shattering:

Nehemiah 1:11 *O Lord, I beseech thee, let now thine ear be attentive to the prayer of thy servant, and to the prayer of thy servants, who desire to fear thy name: and prosper, I pray thee, thy servant this day, and grant him mercy in the sight of this man. For I was the king's cupbearer.*

Notice that very last phrase, *"For I was the king's cupbearer."* Nehemiah wanted to ask the king to be allowed to leave Persia and go to Jerusalem to rebuild the walls. But he was afraid to ask because he was the king's cupbearer. Why would something as mundane as being a cupbearer have anything to do with this issue? Simple: being a "cupbearer" to a king was nothing at all like being a waiter or waitress. That position was the nearest thing to a Vice President that the ancient world knew. The cupbearer was the king's most trusted assistant, the man who literally kept him alive by tasting the contents of his cup before the king did to keep him from being poisoned. The cupbearer, especially to the king of Persia, was powerful, popular, and well-paid. Nehemiah was living in the lap of luxury. He had it all.

And it wasn't enough. As long as God's people had such a dire need to be met, as long as they were suffering and he could possibly help, the entire world would never be enough. Thus, Nehemiah was willing to give up everything to go and help.

DO evaluate your priorities. If we know and love God, then all of the wealth of this world will never be enough when there is a task that He has laid upon our hearts, especially when that task is helping those in need!

Personal Notes:

_____

_____

_____

_____

_____

_____

_____

_____

_____

_____

_____

_____

_____

_____

_____

_____

_____

_____

_____

_____

_____

_____

_____

Devotion 46

As chapter two begins, Nehemiah has been burdened and grieving and praying for approximately three months. He has, as yet, apparently said nothing to the king. But what he could not say with words, his face finally communicated for him, and the king was perceptive enough to see it.

Nehemiah 2:1 *And it came to pass in the month Nisan, in the twentieth year of Artaxerxes the king, that wine was before him: and I took up the wine, and gave it unto the king. Now I had not been beforetime sad in his presence.* **2** *Wherefore the king said unto me, Why is thy countenance sad, seeing thou art not sick? this is nothing else but sorrow of heart. Then I was very sore afraid,* **3** *And said unto the king, Let the king live for ever: why should not my countenance be sad, when the city, the place of my fathers' sepulchres, lieth waste, and the gates thereof are consumed with fire?*

I am intrigued by the statement, "*I had not been beforetime sad in his presence.*" In order for Nehemiah to have achieved this lofty position, he would have had to be known by the king for a very long time. Do you think there is even the remotest chance that over all those long years he had never had an occasion to be sad? Of course not. Therefore, he had simply chosen to not appear sad before the king.

There is a balance to be struck here. When Nehemiah was truly devastated by something, the king saw it written on his face. But through the normal cares and troubles of life, no one saw it on his face. This is not a matter of being disingenuous. It is a realization of two facts. One, on our worst days, God has still been very good to us. Two, moods are contagious, whether positive or negative. If we choose to display joy, others will be joyful, and if we choose to display misery, others will be miserable.

DO make joy your normal choice of life!

Personal Notes:

_____

_____

_____

_____

_____

_____

_____

_____

_____

_____

_____

_____

_____

_____

_____

_____

_____

_____

_____

_____

_____

_____

Devotion 47

The king had noticed the sadness of Nehemiah, and Nehemiah had explained it to him. How could he be anything but sad when the walls and gates of Jerusalem were burned and lying in heaps of rubble?

So now the ball was in the King's court, so to speak. How would he respond to Nehemiah's anguish?

Nehemiah 2:4 *Then the king said unto me, For what dost thou make request? So I prayed to the God of heaven.* **5** *And I said unto the king, If it please the king, and if thy servant have found favour in thy sight, that thou wouldest send me unto Judah, unto the city of my fathers' sepulchres, that I may build it.* **6** *And the king said unto me, (the queen also sitting by him,) For how long shall thy journey be? and when wilt thou return? So it pleased the king to send me; and I set him a time.*

This was a truly remarkable act of graciousness on the part of the king. Jerusalem was not really his problem, but letting his trusted cupbearer leave, his insurance policy against being poisoned, that was his problem! And yet he quickly agreed to do so, asking only how long he would be gone and when he would return.

How amazing is it that such a lesson of Christian graciousness could come from the example of a pagan king! He was saying, in so many words, "If it bothers you, it bothers me. What can I do to help?"

You are likely going to meet hurting people today. DO have that same gracious attitude of, "If it bothers you, it bothers me. What can I do to help?"

Personal Notes:

_____
_____
_____
_____
_____
_____
_____
_____
_____
_____
_____
_____
_____
_____
_____
_____
_____
_____
_____
_____
_____
_____
_____
_____
_____
_____
_____
_____
_____
_____

Devotion 48

Nehemiah had been given permission to go back to Jerusalem and rebuild the walls and gates. But his entourage was going to look vastly different from that of Ezra some fourteen years earlier. Ezra and his company had come with no security whatsoever. Look at how Nehemiah came:

Nehemiah 2:7 *Moreover I said unto the king, If it please the king, let letters be given me to the governors beyond the river, that they may convey me over till I come into Judah;* **8** *And a letter unto Asaph the keeper of the king's forest, that he may give me timber to make beams for the gates of the palace which appertained to the house, and for the wall of the city, and for the house that I shall enter into. And the king granted me, according to the good hand of my God upon me.* **9** *Then I came to the governors beyond the river, and gave them the king's letters. Now the king had sent captains of the army and horsemen with me.*

Captains of the army and horsemen. Yes, Ezra had asked to not have any security because God would protect him, but Nehemiah, it seems, was not even given that option. The king simply decreed that part of the army would go with him to ensure his safe passage! It is very clear that Nehemiah had made himself valuable to the king.

There is some practical wisdom in that. Whether it be with employers, officials, or any other secular authority, believers ought to be so hard-working, dependable, and honorable that even secular people value them! It is a matter of testimony.

DO make yourself valuable to those you serve!

Personal Notes:

_____

_____

_____

_____

_____

_____

_____

_____

_____

_____

_____

_____

_____

_____

_____

_____

_____

_____

_____

_____

_____

_____

_____

_____

_____

_____

_____

Devotion 49

The burned-down and wrecked walls and gates of Jerusalem were about to be rebuilt. That is a wonderful thing and was surely celebrated by everyone, right? That would be a "no."

Nehemiah 2:10 *When Sanballat the Horonite, and Tobiah the servant, the Ammonite, heard of it, it grieved them exceedingly that there was come a man to seek the welfare of the children of Israel.*

We are here introduced to the first two antagonists of the book of Nehemiah. The third one, Geshem, will appear in verse nineteen. These men were exceedingly grieved *"that there was come a man to seek the welfare of the children of Israel."*

Let that sink in. This was not a little thing to them; their world was completely shattered because someone was trying to help the children of Israel, the descendants of Abraham. It is called anti-Semitism, and it has been around for a very long time. Even into our day, there are multitudes of people who genuinely hate the Jews simply because of who they are and because God has chosen them as the apple of His eye. Today we even have them as elected congressmen and congresswomen in the United States of America. College campuses and big corporations proudly shout "BDS!" meaning boycott, divest, and sanction, their way of trying to bankrupt the nation of Israel.

It was wicked then, and it is still wicked today. The heroes of the Book of Nehemiah were for the Jews; the enemies of the Book of Nehemiah were against them.

DO recognize anti-Semitism for the devilish doctrine that it is!

Personal Notes:

_____

_____

_____

_____

_____

_____

_____

_____

_____

_____

_____

_____

_____

_____

_____

_____

_____

_____

_____

_____

_____

_____

_____

_____

_____

_____

Devotion 50

Just as Ezra had done after his trip from Persia to Jerusalem, Nehemiah rested for three days when he arrived. And then he got up and did some survey work.

Nehemiah 2:12 *And I arose in the night, I and some few men with me; neither told I any man what my God had put in my heart to do at Jerusalem: neither was there any beast with me, save the beast that I rode upon.* **13** *And I went out by night by the gate of the valley, even before the dragon well, and to the dung port, and viewed the walls of Jerusalem, which were broken down, and the gates thereof were consumed with fire.* **14** *Then I went on to the gate of the fountain, and to the king's pool: but there was no place for the beast that was under me to pass.* **15** *Then went I up in the night by the brook, and viewed the wall, and turned back, and entered by the gate of the valley, and so returned.* **16** *And the rulers knew not whither I went, or what I did; neither had I as yet told it to the Jews, nor to the priests, nor to the nobles, nor to the rulers, nor to the rest that did the work.*

For three days, this clearly important figure from the palaces of Persia was in Jerusalem, and no one even knew why. Then he got up at night, when there would be no prying eyes to see what he was up to, and did an extensive viewing of the damage. It would only be after this that he would say anything at all about why he was there and what he had in mind.

In other words, even though he had heard about the situation from a "trusted source," he would not actually comment on it to his people until he had seen it for himself and knew exactly what to say.

Nehemiah would have been lousy at social media.

DO learn the wisdom of not speaking until you know!

Personal Notes:

_____

_____

_____

_____

_____

_____

_____

_____

_____

_____

_____

_____

_____

_____

_____

_____

_____

_____

_____

_____

_____

_____

_____

_____

Devotion 51

The story is told that one fine day, The Lone Ranger and Tonto, his loyal companion, were riding through a canyon when suddenly, a band of fierce Apache warriors appeared, lining the rim of both sides of the canyon. There must have been a thousand arrows pointed their way, with bowstrings pulled back, just waiting for the command to fire.

The Lone Ranger looked at Tonto and said, "What are we going to do?"

Tonto merely edged his horse a few feet away from The Lone Ranger and said, "Whadda ya mean 'we,' white boy?"

Nehemiah had surveyed the damage, and now he was ready to tell everyone what was on his heart. As he did, he used a few very small but powerful words.

Nehemiah 2:17 *Then said I unto them, Ye see the distress that WE are in, how Jerusalem lieth waste, and the gates thereof are burned with fire: come, and let US build up the wall of Jerusalem, that WE be no more a reproach.*

Nehemiah did not have to be there, and everyone knew it. He could have looked at the damage, decided it was more trouble than he wanted to get into, and left. But by using we, us, and we, he let them know that they really were all in it together. And they quickly got that message:

Nehemiah 2:18 *Then I told them of the hand of my God which was good upon me; as also the king's words that he had spoken unto me. And they said, Let*

106

US rise up and build. So they strengthened their hands for this good work.

Telling people what to do will never be anywhere near as powerful as getting in there with them and putting your own hands to the work. "We" will always be more powerful than "you."

DO use the power of WE!

Personal Notes:

_____

_____

_____

_____

_____

_____

_____

_____

_____

_____

_____

_____

_____

_____

_____

_____

_____

_____

_____

_____

_____

_____

_____

_____

Devotion 52

No true work for God will ever go unchallenged. And sure enough, once Nehemiah convinced everyone to start rebuilding the walls, the three main antagonists of the book reared their ugly (yet probably heavily coiffed and pampered) heads.

Nehemiah 2:19 *But when Sanballat the Horonite, and Tobiah the servant, the Ammonite, and Geshem the Arabian, heard it, they laughed us to scorn, and despised us, and said, What is this thing that ye do? will ye rebel against the king?*

They laughed, they despised, and they accused. The one thing they did not do, though, was ask. If they had, they would have known that Nehemiah was actually doing what he did with the express permission of the king. But since they did not ask, he clearly was not inclined to tell them, preferring instead to just let them remain ignorant. But he did answer them back, and forcefully.

Nehemiah 2:20 *Then answered I them, and said unto them, The God of heaven, he will prosper us; therefore we his servants will arise and build: but ye have no portion, nor right, nor memorial, in Jerusalem.*

Nehemiah answered these enemies by listing three things they did not have in Jerusalem, the city whose walls were about to be rebuilt. Those three things were any portion, right, or memorial. In other words, they were not from there, had not been given any of it by God, had invested nothing in it through the years, and therefore, had no business at all in the matter.

If I could put this in simple terms, "No skin in the game, no seat at the table."

DO be willing to extend a hand of friendship when it is warranted, but DO be equally willing to extend a (hopefully figurative) palm to the face when that is warranted!

Personal Notes:

_____

_____

_____

_____

_____

_____

_____

_____

_____

_____

_____

_____

_____

_____

_____

_____

_____

_____

_____

_____

_____

_____

Devotion 53

The goal of Nehemiah in coming all the way from Persia was to rebuild the walls of Jerusalem. And all of chapter three is about that rebuilding process, who engaged in it, and what part they rebuilt. It is the kind of chapter people are often tempted just to skim over and get past so they can get to "the good stuff" elsewhere. And that would be a big mistake because the details of who built what, in this case, are very instructive, and we will spend several days looking at it.

Nehemiah 3:1 *Then Eliashib the high priest rose up with his brethren the priests, and they builded the sheep gate; they sanctified it, and set up the doors of it; even unto the tower of Meah they sanctified it, unto the tower of Hananeel.*

When you think of the clergy, you likely get a view in your mind of a clean, manicured, well-dressed, soft-spoken man who has never had a blister a day in his life. And that is a crying shame because the priests in this verse set a much better example. The very first people listed as building part of the wall were the clergy right there in Jerusalem! Yes, every preacher should spend time on their knees and behind a desk, but unless they are physically infirmed or too old to help, they should never view themselves as too good to "minister" with a hammer or saw or tape measure or mop or broom or plunger for that matter.

You who are in the ministry or are going into the ministry, DO be willing to "build the wall" along with everyone else!

Personal Notes:

Devotion 54

As we continue looking at the individuals and groups who rebuilt different portions of the wall of Jerusalem under the leadership of Nehemiah, we come to a group that, to put it mildly, was pretty pathetic.

Nehemiah 3:5 *And next unto them the Tekoites repaired; but their nobles put not their necks to the work of their Lord.*

The "nobles" of Tekoa felt like menial labor was beneath them. What sorry, worthless skin sacks!

If we are "too good" to sweep or mop or change poopy diapers or hold doors or vacuum floors or show up to workdays, then there is really nothing "noble" about us. If we rightly take Christ for the example of real nobility, we will find One who left heaven for Earth, provided and served lunch for thousands, helped fishermen gather their daily haul, held dirty little children in His arms, and washed the stinky, sweaty, smelly feet of 12 men, one of whom was right then in the process of betraying Him.

But even in that wall-building project many years before the time of Christ, those in Jerusalem still had an example of true nobility, a man named Nehemiah who left the beautiful palace to labor in the building project.

DO evaluate your true nobility; if your hands are too good to hold a plunger, you have none.

Personal Notes:

Devotion 55

Quick! Say out loud an occupation of the person least likely to be involved in a heavy, sweaty, dirty, backbreaking building project like rebuilding the wall of the city...

What is your answer? Mine would probably be something like "doctor."

Look with me, please, at another group of people involved in the rebuilding of the wall of Jerusalem.

Nehemiah 3:8 *Next unto him repaired Uzziel the son of Harhaiah, of the goldsmiths. Next unto him also repaired Hananiah the son of one of the apothecaries, and they fortified Jerusalem unto the broad wall.*

Goldsmiths then, like now, are jewelers, people who make lovely, delicate items out of gold. Apothecaries were basically perfume makers. That is also a very delicate, clean, high-end kind of occupation. And yet here we find goldsmiths and apothecaries doing masonry work, rebuilding portions of the wall. In other words, these people were willing to step outside of their job description and even outside of their comfort zone to see the work of the Lord move forward.

What an excellent example! All of us have a job description of some kind, and all of us have a comfort zone. And yet, if anything great is ever going to be done for God, we must be willing, if necessary, to move beyond those things in order to see the job done.

DO view the cause of Christ as more important than a comfort zone!

Personal Notes:

_____

_____

_____

_____

_____

_____

_____

_____

_____

_____

_____

_____

_____

_____

_____

_____

_____

_____

_____

_____

_____

_____

_____

_____

_____

Devotion 56

As we continue looking at the list of people and groups who helped to rebuild the broken-down walls of Jerusalem, we come to a man with a funny-sounding family name who can teach us a serious truth.

Nehemiah 3:10 *And next unto them repaired Jedaiah the son of Harumaph, even over against his house.*

Jedaiah the son of "Harumaph." Jedaiah, the guy whose father's name sounds like an exasperated sound: Tom: "Hey, Bob, your team really got stomped yesterday!" Bob: "Harumaph!"

In seriousness, though, Jedaiah repaired the part of the wall that joined to his own house. Was this a selfish move on his part? Hardly; if that portion of the wall was not repaired, the entire city was at risk due to the breach, not just Jedaiah and his family. And what it should remind us of today is the folly and hypocrisy of pointing out the "gaps" in the lives and homes of others but not recognizing or repairing our own! It is very easy to see all the flaws of "those people" and to have all the answers for how to fix them. It is much harder to see our own flaws and do what is necessary to correct them for the good of everyone.

DO repair any of your own "broken sections of wall!"

Personal Notes:

_____
_____
_____
_____
_____
_____
_____
_____
_____
_____
_____
_____
_____
_____
_____
_____
_____
_____
_____
_____
_____
_____
_____
_____
_____
_____
_____
_____
_____
_____
_____

Devotion 57

Moving further down in the list of those people and groups who helped to repair the broken-down walls of Jerusalem, we come to some folks who are "pretty" eye-opening and should put a big smile on our faces.

Nehemiah 3:12 *And next unto him repaired Shallum the son of Halohesh, the ruler of the half part of Jerusalem, he and his daughters.*

When we think of demolition and heavy construction, I would surmise that few people have the word "daughters" come to mind. That is normally the work of big, strong men. But with enemies gathering all around them, the situation was dire, and these precious girls stepped up to work like full-grown men in an hour of need, and they were led by their father in doing so.

His sons are not mentioned. It very much seems as though this man never had any boys, therefore, but raised girls who were as good as any boys and just as willing to get dirt under their fingernails if that is what it took to get the wall done. There is something amazing about a girl who is feminine, pretty, proper, and at the same time can haul block if it comes right down to it!

Girls, DO be feminine, but DO also have the ability and the willingness to "do the dirty work" when the need arises!

Personal Notes:

_____

_____

_____

_____

_____

_____

_____

_____

_____

_____

_____

_____

_____

_____

_____

_____

_____

_____

_____

_____

_____

_____

_____

_____

_____

_____

_____

_____

_____

_____

_____

_____

Devotion 58

Moving even further into the list of people who helped to rebuild the broken-down walls of Jerusalem, we come across some of the most productive members in the entire project.

Nehemiah 3:13 *The valley gate repaired Hanun, and the inhabitants of Zanoah; they built it, and set up the doors thereof, the locks thereof, and the bars thereof, and a thousand cubits on the wall unto the dung gate.*

These men repaired the gate and installed the doors and locks and bars on it, all of which was very specialized work. Even today, all of that is specialized work. They also repaired 1,500 feet of the wall, an enormous amount of work. Many people did all they could do, even though all they could do was a small amount. These folks did all they could do, and it was a huge amount.

There will always be people that God has blessed to be able to do massive amounts of work for Him. Without people like that, the work of God would not go nearly as far as fast. The key is for everyone to do as much as they possibly can for God and neither resent those who cannot do as much nor get jealous of those who can do more!

DO as much as you possibly can for God, and DO rejoice both over what you can do and what others are able to do!

Personal Notes:

_____
_____
_____
_____
_____
_____
_____
_____
_____
_____
_____
_____
_____
_____
_____
_____
_____
_____
_____
_____
_____
_____
_____
_____
_____
_____
_____
_____
_____

Devotion 59

Quick! What is the first thing that pops into your head when I ask you this question, "Where would you really NOT want to work?"

My answer would probably be, "In a cubicle somewhere doing monotonous paperwork."

But let me show you a very important man who found himself working very hard in a very undesirable place in Nehemiah's wall-building project.

Nehemiah 3:14 *But the dung gate repaired Malchiah the son of Rechab, the ruler of part of Bethhaccerem; he built it, and set up the doors thereof, the locks thereof, and the bars thereof.*

Malchiah was a ruler, a very important man. But he ended up repairing the dung gate and its doors and locks and bars. As you might surmise by the name, this was a filthy, smelly place to be working. This was where all of the trash and animal poop of the city came through to be dumped in the valley. If there was ever a place where pretty much no one wanted to work, that would be it. And yet, it was just as necessary to be repaired as everywhere else.

So this important man stepped up to the task and worked in a very literal "poopy place" and got the job done.

Sometimes God may have us serving in polished places; sometimes, He may have us serving in poopy places. But either way, we are not serving for the place; we are serving for the God who put us there! So DO give your all, whether in polished places or poopy places!

Personal Notes:

Devotion 60

As the list of those who helped Nehemiah in rebuilding the walls of Jerusalem continues, we come to a contrast between two different kinds of workers.

Nehemiah 3:19 *And next to him repaired Ezer the son of Jeshua, the ruler of Mizpah, another piece over against the going up to the armoury at the turning of the wall.* **20** *After him Baruch the son of Zabbai earnestly repaired the other piece, from the turning of the wall unto the door of the house of Eliashib the high priest.*

Look at Ezer in verse nineteen and Baruch in verse twenty, and see if you can find one word that marks the difference between them...

Insert Jeopardy theme song, Doo doo doo doo doo doo doo, doo doo doo doo DOO, doo doo doo doo doo...

Earnestly. Ezer did his assigned part of the work, but Baruch "*earnestly repaired the other piece.*" Not one thing is listed as a negative about Ezer and his work or work ethic, but Baruch stood out from him and others because he "earnestly" did his work. In other words, there was a look of determination on his face; he got at it earlier than others; he stayed at it later than others; he was thoroughly passionate about getting this job done.

Shouldn't that be the kind of testimony that every Christian develops?

In a world that is already preconditioned to believe that Christians are lazy and inept, DO prove them wrong with an "earnest" work ethic!

Personal Notes:

_____
_____
_____
_____
_____
_____
_____
_____
_____
_____
_____
_____
_____
_____
_____
_____
_____
_____
_____
_____
_____
_____
_____
_____
_____
_____
_____

Devotion 61

There are no errors in your Bible. Because of that, it means what it says, not what some wish or assume that it means. That is pretty important to understand as we begin to look at the next group of people listed in the wall-building project.

Nehemiah 3:26 *Moreover the Nethinims dwelt in Ophel, unto the place over against the water gate toward the east, and the tower that lieth out.*

For twenty-five verses now, we have been reading the words "repaired" and "builded." Those words occur in nearly every single verse. But neither of them occurs in verse twenty-six.

When we come to the Nethinims, we simply read that they "dwelt" in Ophel. The text does not say that they repaired or built anything; it simply tells us that they lived there. It very much seems as though they were not quite the same as when they returned with Ezra, they enjoyed the benefits of all that was going on, and they also enjoyed not having to labor for all of those benefits! In today's world, we call that mentality "freeloading." And it is a mentality that should never be found amongst the children of God.

It is very easy to sit back and let everyone else do the work and then criticize how the work is done. Very few things through the many years of my ministry have made me come close to losing control of "the fist of death" quite like this! It has not happened often, and not for a very long time, but there is nothing more frustrating than a freeloader who criticizes the back he or she is riding on.

DO more than just come along for the ride; DO help to pull the cart!

Personal Notes:

_____

_____

_____

_____

_____

_____

_____

_____

_____

_____

_____

_____

_____

_____

_____

_____

_____

_____

_____

_____

_____

_____

_____

_____

_____

_____

_____

Devotion 62

A beautiful two-word phrase occurs in verse twenty-seven as we continue to read the account of the rebuilding of the wall.

Nehemiah 3:27 *After them the Tekoites repaired another piece, over against the great tower that lieth out, even unto the wall of Ophel.*

Another piece. We have already read of the Tekoites and their work of rebuilding the wall back in verse five, where we found that *"they repaired, but their nobles put not their necks to the work of their Lord."* The Tekoites were the hard workers with the horrible leaders. And that is what makes what we read in verse twenty-seven so very remarkable. These people not only repaired their section in verse five, but they also moved on to repair another piece of the wall as well!

Have you ever had the frustration of having to deal with either a child or an employee to whom you would give a task, and if they did the task, they would then quietly disappear until you came looking for them? That is incredibly frustrating and a sign of either immaturity or incredibly poor character. When it comes to the work of the Lord, until the entire task is done, "our part" should never be regarded as done! In other words, we should not have the mentality that says, "What is the least amount that I can get by with doing?" We should have the mentality that says, "If I have gotten done my piece of the work, who can I help to finish their part of the work?"

Don't just be a "bare minimum servant" of the Lord; do your part, and then see if there is someone else that you can help to do their part!

Personal Notes:

_____

_____

_____

_____

_____

_____

_____

_____

_____

_____

_____

_____

_____

_____

_____

_____

_____

_____

_____

_____

_____

_____

_____

_____

_____

Devotion 63

At the end of chapter three, we finally arrive full circle, literally, in the list of those repairing the wall of Jerusalem.

Nehemiah 3:31 *After him repaired Malchiah the goldsmith's son unto the place of the Nethinims, and of the merchants, over against the gate Miphkad, and to the going up of the corner.* **32** *And between the going up of the corner unto the sheep gate repaired the goldsmiths and the merchants.*

These men had the privilege of being the closers. They got to repair the last piece.

Many men in this chapter did not have anything specific said about them other than that "they repaired." They are just as important as all the rest. They did not all repair 1,500 feet, but everyone who actually dug in and worked played a vital role in getting the entire thing done.

There is something for everyone to do in serving God. Not everyone can stand behind the pulpit, but everyone can and should do something. So here's a question: If God were writing one more chapter of Scripture about the work of God going on in your church, what would He write, or not write, about you?

DO make sure that your service would give God something to "write home about!"

Personal Notes:

Devotion 64

The great work of rebuilding the wall was not going to be able to be hidden from the enemies of God and his people. And sure enough...

Nehemiah 4:1 *But it came to pass, that when Sanballat heard that we builded the wall, he was wroth, and took great indignation, and mocked the Jews.* **2** *And he spake before his brethren and the army of Samaria, and said, What do these feeble Jews? will they fortify themselves? will they sacrifice? will they make an end in a day? will they revive the stones out of the heaps of the rubbish which are burned?*

Aren't the blessings that you see in those verses amazing? It kind of makes you want to shout and run laps and scream, "Glory to God" at the top of your lungs!

No, I have not lost my mind. There really is a huge blessing in these verses. Sanballat was really seriously angry that the wall was being rebuilt. But his response was to go there and mock them over it. His response was to make fun of them. In other words, rather than gather a military force to try to stop them immediately, he underestimated them and simply made fun of them. That tactical error on his part gave them time to get the wall much more complete and the defenses much more organized before the threat of physical violence finally came.

Many times the things that we despise, things like people making fun of us, are actually blessings from the hand of our all-knowing God.

DO be perceptive enough to understand that sometimes the things that bother us are the very things that are helping to preserve us from far worse things!

Personal Notes:

_____

_____

_____

_____

_____

_____

_____

_____

_____

_____

_____

_____

_____

_____

_____

_____

_____

_____

_____

_____

_____

_____

_____

_____

_____

_____

_____

_____

Devotion 65

We now arrive at one of the most important verses in the entire book of Nehemiah in terms of practical help for us today.

Nehemiah 4:6 *So built we the wall; and all the wall was joined together unto the half thereof: for the people had a mind to work.*

In a very short period of time, the entire wall was joined together and was at half of its intended height. This was an enormous project. They had no heavy equipment, no dump trucks, no bulldozers, no cranes. Everything was done by hand. As far as the enemy could see, they were right in their ridicule. There was nothing that the Jews had that the enemy could see that would allow them to complete such a project. But there was one thing they had that the enemy could not see that more than made up for the things that they did not have: a mind to work.

A "mind to work" is really more important than a "working mind." In other words, effort is more important than intelligence. Both are important, but one is actually more important than the other. You can be a genius, but if you are lazy, it will do you no good whatsoever. But on the other hand, you can have the intelligence of a broad-leaf weed, and if you will buckle down and go to work, you will get more done than the lazy genius ever will.

DO have a mind to work!

Personal Notes:

Devotion 66

We saw just a couple of devotions ago that the enemies of God made a tactical error by underestimating them and simply mocking them for what they were doing. Finally, they realized that error and did what, on a practical level, they should have done at the very first.

Nehemiah 4:7 *But it came to pass, that when Sanballat, and Tobiah, and the Arabians, and the Ammonites, and the Ashdodites, heard that the walls of Jerusalem were made up, and that the breaches began to be stopped, then they were very wroth,* **8** *And conspired all of them together to come and to fight against Jerusalem, and to hinder it.*

We have already heard of Sanballat and Tobiah and Geshem and the Arabians and the Ammonites as enemies of God in this book. But now the Ashdodites are added to the mix. Ashdod was one of the five chief cities of the Philistines.

Isn't it amazing how enemies are a lot like rabbits in the way they multiply?

But here is the good news. Those enemies were only multiplying because God's people were making progress. The devil is many things, but stupid is not one of those things. He does not send an entire legion of demons to deal with one "Christian" in the middle of nowhere who never goes to church and cannot remember where his Bible is. If he is "hitting you with all he has got," then you are making progress whether it seems like it or not!

DO remember that the shells only start flying when you are over the target!

Personal Notes:

_____

_____

_____

_____

_____

_____

_____

_____

_____

_____

_____

_____

_____

_____

_____

_____

_____

_____

_____

_____

_____

_____

_____

_____

_____

_____

_____

_____

_____

Devotion 67

Enemies were now gathering around Jerusalem, intent on stopping the rebuilding of the walls by physical force and violence. What would you do under such circumstances? Nehemiah knew just the thing.

Nehemiah 4:9 *Nevertheless we made our prayer unto our God, and set a watch against them day and night, because of them.*

There is a fascinating combination of words in that verse, prayer and watch. We find them together several other times in Scripture from the mouth of Jesus Himself. Here is one of those times:

Matthew 26:41 *Watch and pray, that ye enter not into temptation: the spirit indeed is willing, but the flesh is weak.*

Here, as well, is another verse from the book of Proverbs that teaches the same thing in slightly different words:

Proverbs 21:31 *The horse is prepared against the day of battle: but safety is of the LORD.*

What does all of this tell us? We must pray, but we must also watch. We must know that safety is of the Lord; we must also prepare the horse unto the day of battle. One is never complete without the other. Prayers are the wings, but they also need feet. Nehemiah prayed AND set a watch; he trusted God fully AND also gave maximum effort.

Whatever trial or task you face, DO both watch and pray; DO trust and try!

Personal Notes:

_____
_____
_____
_____
_____
_____
_____
_____
_____
_____
_____
_____
_____
_____
_____
_____
_____
_____
_____
_____
_____
_____
_____
_____
_____
_____
_____
_____
_____
_____

Devotion 68

Nehemiah and the builders had been facing the discouragement of outward attack trying to get them to stop building the wall. They set a watch and prayed, and that was dealt with. But then came another source of discouragement, this time from internal sources.

Nehemiah 4:10 *And Judah said, The strength of the bearers of burdens is decayed, and there is much rubbish; so that we are not able to build the wall.*

There were some people whose task was to carry away the rubbish from the old wall and from the materials employed in building the new wall. Those people were exhausted. They believed they could not carry off even one more block. Because of that and the amount of rubbish left to move, they had reached a point where the building project had come to a standstill. And then, to make matters worse, a fresh round of threats came from outside, ten separate instances where the enemy threatened to attack them from directions they could not see.

Nehemiah addressed those security risks. He put warriors in place, and he motivated them to fight. But he did not address the assertion that not one more block could be moved. Instead...

Nehemiah 4:15 *...we returned all of us to the wall, every one unto his work.*

They simply got back to work. The solution to the problem of "We cannot possibly move another block" was to go out and move a few more blocks, then a few more, then a few more. You see, they did not have to do everything all at once; they just had to do the next thing in front of them. Just by doing that, everything would eventually be done.

When you get overwhelmed by the magnitude of all that is in front of you, DO just "pick up the next block!"

Personal Notes:

_____

_____

_____

_____

_____

_____

_____

_____

_____

_____

_____

_____

_____

_____

_____

_____

_____

_____

_____

_____

_____

_____

_____

Devotion 69

We now come to a portion of the text that is both hilarious and instructive.

Nehemiah 4:17 *They which builded on the wall, and they that bare burdens, with those that laded, every one with one of his hands wrought in the work, and with the other hand held a weapon.* **18** *For the builders, every one had his sword girded by his side, and so builded. And he that sounded the trumpet was by me.*

Picture this. You and a few friends, henchmen of the local evil villain, have been sent to harass and attack some construction workers and stop the project. You arrive at your destination and shout at a guy, "Hey, Bub, turn around look me in the face!" and he does so. As he does, you notice that he is holding a sledgehammer in one hand and a loaded .45 in the other.

"What can I do for you?" he asks pleasantly.

To which you suddenly feel the urge to reply, "Could you tell us where the local Girl Scout troop is? I have a sudden desire for some Thin Mints..."

By having each of the workers there in Jerusalem carry a weapon in one hand and a tool in the other, Nehemiah was sending this message; "We can do this the easy way, or we can do this the hard way. Either way is fine with us; you choose."

A person without the capacity to be dangerous is not virtuous; he or she is a victim waiting to happen. Nehemiah understood that while building is preferable, sometimes battling is necessary, and he prepared and equipped his people for either or both.

DO be willing and able to both build and battle!

Personal Notes:

_____

_____

_____

_____

_____

_____

_____

_____

_____

_____

_____

_____

_____

_____

_____

_____

_____

_____

_____

_____

_____

_____

_____

_____

_____

_____

_____

_____

Devotion 70

Moment by moment, Nehemiah made adjustments and preparations as necessary for what they were facing as they tried to defend themselves and build the wall simultaneously. And here was the next thing he put in place for that dual purpose.

Nehemiah 4:19 *And I said unto the nobles, and to the rulers, and to the rest of the people, The work is great and large, and we are separated upon the wall, one far from another.* **20** *In what place therefore ye hear the sound of the trumpet, resort ye thither unto us: our God shall fight for us.*

For me, reading these verses always evokes the image in my mind of some "Lord of the Rings Battle" where a guy trying to hold off thirty orcs is blowing the trumpet, and people are rushing to his aid. That is, in fact, (other than the orcs) the very kind of thing that Nehemiah had in mind.

Our work, as believers today, is much the same as Nehemiah's work of rebuilding the wall, "the work is great and large, and we are separated far from each other." Everyone tends to get caught up in their own lives, their own plans, their own issues, and their own battles. But as believers, it really is true that "We are all in this thing together!" That being the case, we should both be willing to blow the trumpet for help when we need it and also be willing to run to give help when others are the ones blowing the trumpet.

DO be willing to blow the trumpet or respond to the trumpet as needed!

Personal Notes:

_____
_____
_____
_____
_____
_____
_____
_____
_____
_____
_____
_____
_____
_____
_____
_____
_____
_____
_____
_____
_____
_____
_____
_____
_____
_____
_____
_____

Devotion 71

Nehemiah and company were very serious about accomplishing the task at hand. So much so that they were even willing to "make a bit of a stink about it."

Nehemiah 4:23 *So neither I, nor my brethren, nor my servants, nor the men of the guard which followed me, none of us put off our clothes, saving that every one put them off for washing.*

They slept in their clothing. They worked in their clothing. They kept the same things on for days and days and days until they just had to stop and wash them, and then they did it all over again. Comfort was irrelevant; there was a job to do. They would doubtless have been derided as "the clothespin on the nose people," but their dedication to the task got the job done where others had not even been willing to try because of the great magnitude of the work.

Normal effort produces normal results; great efforts produce great results. If anyone on earth ought to understand that and apply it regularly, it is the people of God. Our King made a great effort coming from heaven to earth and being born in the flesh and living a perfect and sinless life and dying on Calvary for us and rising from the dead on the third day. No one ever gave a greater effort to a task than He did. And if we are to truly be like Him, our lives should also be marked by great effort at great tasks.

DO be a person who goes above and beyond the call of dirty, I mean, "duty!"

Personal Notes:

Devotion 72

Here is the situation thus far in the book of Nehemiah. The people had just recently come back from captivity. The walls were destroyed, the city burned, and they all had to spend their days trying to fix it. There were enemies all around threatening to destroy them. So, in addition to having to work on the walls all day, they were also having to hold swords and weapons and stand guard all day and night lest they be overrun. It was a time of great emergencies; these people were just trying to stay alive. But, as is so often the case, problems seem to beget more problems.

Nehemiah 5:1 *And there was a great cry of the people and of their wives against their brethren the Jews. 2 For there were that said, We, our sons, and our daughters, are many: therefore we take up corn for them, that we may eat, and live. 3 Some also there were that said, We have mortgaged our lands, vineyards, and houses, that we might buy corn, because of the dearth. 4 There were also that said, We have borrowed money for the king's tribute, and that upon our lands and vineyards.*

In simple language, in addition to the other problems they were facing, they were also experiencing a drought; they were having to take out loans to buy food for their families, some of them were even mortgaging their homes and lands just for groceries, and they were even having to borrow money to pay their taxes. But then we read this that really gets to the heart of the problem:

Nehemiah 5:5 *Yet now our flesh is as the flesh of our brethren, our children as their children: and, lo, we bring into bondage our sons and our daughters to be servants, and some of our daughters are brought unto bondage already: neither is it in our power to redeem them; for other men have our lands and vineyards.*

In a time of great national need when everyone was supposed to be working together, wealthy individuals were taking their own poor countrymen into servitude. They were making a huge profit off of the misery of others.

Is there anything wrong with making a profit? Certainly not. But is there anything right about gouging others in a time of disaster? Again, certainly not. Profit is fine; profiteering is not.

DO see more than dollar signs when you look at people!

Personal Notes:

_____
_____
_____
_____
_____
_____
_____
_____
_____
_____
_____
_____

Devotion 73

The poor people of the land, suffering both under attacks from without and drought from above and, to make matters much worse, people trafficking in their misery from within, went to Nehemiah for help. And the way he responded is both instructive and a bit hilarious.

Nehemiah 5:6 *And I was very angry when I heard their cry and these words.* **7** *Then I consulted with myself, and I rebuked the nobles, and the rulers, and said unto them, Ye exact usury, every one of his brother. And I set a great assembly against them.*

The first thing we notice is that Nehemiah got "very angry." Not just angry, VERY angry. He was absolutely livid. You will often be told by misinformed "theologians" that Christians should never get angry. But that is clearly an erroneous view. Nehemiah got very angry; even Jesus got very angry. There are some things that are definitely worth getting angry over, and a person without the capacity to get angry is not a good person; he or she is simply a weak person.

But the second thing to notice is that when Nehemiah got angry, he *"consulted with myself."* It means exactly what you think it means; Nehemiah was literally talking to himself! "Well, what are we going to do now? I'll tell you what we are going to do, we are going to clean their stinking clocks; that's what we are going to do!"

His anger and his consultation then led to a confrontation. It was not enough to be angry, nor was it enough simply to say that he was going to do something about it; it was only enough when he put all of that into action.

DO get angry when it is warranted, DO take the next step and "talk it over with yourself to make sure you get everything right in your head," but then definitely DO take action, otherwise the first two steps are of no value whatsoever!

Personal Notes:

_____

_____

_____

_____

_____

_____

_____

_____

_____

_____

_____

_____

_____

_____

_____

_____

_____

_____

_____

_____

Devotion 74

After Nehemiah chewed out the people who were buying and selling their own countrymen in such a time of great national trial, the next verse shows us one of the most remarkable things you will ever see amongst humanity, and it also gives us the "why."

Nehemiah 5:8 *And I said unto them, We after our ability have redeemed our brethren the Jews, which were sold unto the heathen; and will ye even sell your brethren? or shall they be sold unto us? Then held they their peace, and found nothing to answer.*

How many times have you ever personally scolded someone for something they were doing wrong with the result of that being that they simply sat there quietly and took it without answering back for themselves in any way? My guess is, "Almost never!" In my more than fifty years of life thus far, I can only think of a tiny handful of times that has ever happened when I have had to scold someone. People are very much predisposed to answering back and trying to justify any wrong things they are doing.

So how did it work out this way for Nehemiah? What is the "why?" The answer to that is found in the first part of the verse. Nehemiah was able to point out that he and those who came with him were equally financially able to traffic in the misery of their own countrymen but had not done so. In fact, they had taken money out of their own wallets to buy back those of their countrymen who had already been sold to the heathens! In other words, if his argument had just been an argument, they could have argued with his argument. But since his argument was backed up by the way he had already conducted himself, they could not answer back a single word.

If you want people to listen to your arguments, DO spend more time in crafting better conduct than you do in crafting a better argument!

Personal Notes:

_____
_____
_____
_____
_____
_____
_____
_____
_____
_____
_____
_____
_____
_____
_____
_____
_____
_____
_____
_____
_____
_____

Devotion 75

Seeing that the people were quietly listening to what he had to say rather than answering back in protest, Nehemiah pushed ahead until he got the final result that he wanted.

Nehemiah 5:9 *Also I said, It is not good that ye do: ought ye not to walk in the fear of our God because of the reproach of the heathen our enemies?* **10** *I likewise, and my brethren, and my servants, might exact of them money and corn: I pray you, let us leave off this usury.* **11** *Restore, I pray you, to them, even this day, their lands, their vineyards, their oliveyards, and their houses, also the hundredth part of the money, and of the corn, the wine, and the oil, that ye exact of them.* **12** *Then said they, We will restore them, and will require nothing of them; so will we do as thou sayest. Then I called the priests, and took an oath of them, that they should do according to this promise.* **13** *Also I shook my lap, and said, So God shake out every man from his house, and from his labour, that performeth not this promise, even thus be he shaken out, and emptied. And all the congregation said, Amen, and praised the LORD. And the people did according to this promise.*

Nehemiah was too wise simply to leave this as, "Okay, we will do what you said." Instead, he specified in great detail exactly what he wanted, got them to swear an oath before the priests that they would obey, and then invoked the judgment of God if they backed down on their vow. And the end result of all of that was, "The people did according to this promise."

This is called "putting some teeth in it." Oftentimes we ask people to do right, yet we put no teeth in it in case they do wrong. Little wonder then that people often agree to do right and then turn right around and do wrong!

In any situation where you have some control and some authority, DO put teeth into everything important moral thing that you expect people to do; a toothless authority will usually end up as a frustrated authority!

Personal Notes:

_____
_____
_____
_____
_____
_____
_____
_____
_____
_____
_____
_____
_____
_____
_____
_____
_____
_____

Devotion 76

Verse fourteen to the end of the chapter is Nehemiah putting into writing a further account of how he had conducted himself through all of this. Here is a bit of what we find:

Nehemiah 5:14 *Moreover from the time that I was appointed to be their governor in the land of Judah, from the twentieth year even unto the two and thirtieth year of Artaxerxes the king, that is, twelve years, I and my brethren have not eaten the bread of the governor.* **15** *But the former governors that had been before me were chargeable unto the people, and had taken of them bread and wine, beside forty shekels of silver; yea, even their servants bare rule over the people: but so did not I, because of the fear of God.*

The "bread of the governor" Nehemiah referred to was the rather luxurious salary of daily bread and wine and forty shekels of silver. That was a high-dollar salary, especially considering how badly things were going in the country economically. The people who were governors before Nehemiah took that full salary and even put their servants in ruling positions over the people.

Nehemiah did not. He refused to even take a salary for twelve years of work! He lived off of his own savings and did not take a salary. In Persia, he had clearly gladly received all of his large salary. But the situation in Jerusalem was so very different that it warranted a different type of choice. And Nehemiah was a man who was willing to do a good job whether he was able to take a salary from the job or not. In other words, the money was never the main issue for him; the task was the main issue.

While money is important and there is nothing wrong with earning a paycheck, DO always regard the "task" as more important than the "take" and be willing to act accordingly!

Personal Notes:

_____

_____

_____

_____

_____

_____

_____

_____

_____

_____

_____

_____

_____

_____

_____

_____

_____

_____

_____

_____

_____

_____

_____

Devotion 77

As chapter six begins, the internal problems have been dealt with, and the focus turns once again to external problems. The enemies were still there, and now they had a brand-new approach to how to stop the work.

Nehemiah 6:1 *Now it came to pass, when Sanballat, and Tobiah, and Geshem the Arabian, and the rest of our enemies, heard that I had builded the wall, and that there was no breach left therein; (though at that time I had not set up the doors upon the gates;) 2 That Sanballat and Geshem sent unto me, saying, Come, let us meet together in some one of the villages in the plain of Ono. But they thought to do me mischief. 3 And I sent messengers unto them, saying, I am doing a great work, so that I cannot come down: why should the work cease, whilst I leave it, and come down to you? 4 Yet they sent unto me four times after this sort; and I answered them after the same manner.*

I find it more than just a little bit funny that when Nehemiah's enemies tried to lure him out from behind the walls and into a place where they could successfully attack him, they asked to meet in the plane of "Ono." Yes, I understand that in Hebrew that word does not mean what we think of when we say, "Oh no!" in English, but you have to admit it is still funny. And Nehemiah, for his part, was not having anything to do with it, humor or not. He "oh no'd" their idea four straight times!

But the basis upon which he did so is very instructive; "*I am doing a great work, so that I cannot come down."* There is definitely something to learn there. If the enemy cannot destroy the work, he will attempt to delay the work, even using "diplomacy" to do it. But the end result of delay will always end up right where it started, at "destroy!"

DO be leery of any delay in doing what God wants you to do; the devil is just as happy destroying the work by a two-step methodology as he is destroying it by a one-step methodology!

Personal Notes:

_____

_____

_____

_____

_____

_____

_____

_____

_____

_____

_____

_____

_____

_____

_____

_____

_____

_____

_____

_____

Devotion 78

Since Nehemiah said, "Oh no!" to going down to Ono, Sanballat and company switched their attack to yet another methodology to try and stop the work.

Nehemiah 6:5 *Then sent Sanballat his servant unto me in like manner the fifth time with an open letter in his hand;* **6** *Wherein was written, It is reported among the heathen, and Gashmu saith it, that thou and the Jews think to rebel: for which cause thou buildest the wall, that thou mayest be their king, according to these words.* **7** *And thou hast also appointed prophets to preach of thee at Jerusalem, saying, There is a king in Judah: and now shall it be reported to the king according to these words. Come now therefore, and let us take counsel together.*

Sanballat, dear, dear Sanballat, was so concerned that people were talking and might ruin Nehemiah's reputation! The accusation was a serious one—namely that Nehemiah was building the wall so that he could lead the Jews in a rebellion against the king of Persia and become king himself over the Jews there in Israel. But if the concern had been genuine, Sanballat himself could have stopped all the talking since he was the ringleader, and his source, Gashmu, was the very same Geshem that had already been harassing Nehemiah along with Sanballat. When people who are "talking" are concerned about people talking, they actually have very different motives than they are letting on.

DO cast a skeptical eye toward people who are "concerned" about the things that they clearly are not at all concerned about!

Personal Notes:

_____

_____

_____

_____

_____

_____

_____

_____

_____

_____

_____

_____

_____

_____

_____

_____

_____

_____

_____

_____

_____

_____

_____

_____

_____

Devotion 79

Nehemiah had been threatened with the "anonymously sourced complaint." But he quickly rebuffed that and went on with building the wall. Because of that, the devil shifted his strategy one more time.

Nehemiah 6:10 *Afterward I came unto the house of Shemaiah the son of Delaiah the son of Mehetabeel, who was shut up; and he said, Let us meet together in the house of God, within the temple, and let us shut the doors of the temple: for they will come to slay thee; yea, in the night will they come to slay thee.*

This was perhaps the most subtle attack of all. It came from the son of a priest; it came from within the house of God. The tactic was to get Nehemiah to lock himself up in the house of God to secure his own safety. And had he done so, it would have worked! Nehemiah would have been safely locked up behind the walls and shut doors of God's house. The enemy would not have bothered him because he would not have been bothering the enemy! Nehemiah understood this and, in the very next verse, torpedoed that idea.

The devil would love for every one of us to take that option. Just give him the entire world, and he will let us lock ourselves and a few old people inside the walls of the church until we all die off and go away. We will have been safe all the way to the grave, and we will have wasted our entire lives along the way and done nothing at all for God.

DO think more of souls than of safety!

Personal Notes:

_____
_____
_____
_____
_____
_____
_____
_____
_____
_____
_____
_____
_____
_____
_____
_____
_____
_____
_____
_____
_____
_____
_____
_____
_____
_____
_____
_____
_____
_____

Devotion 80

After informing Shemaiah that he would not lock himself away in the house of God, Nehemiah came to a shocking realization.

Nehemiah 6:12 *And, lo, I perceived that God had not sent him; but that he pronounced this prophecy against me: for Tobiah and Sanballat had hired him.* **13** *Therefore was he hired, that I should be afraid, and do so, and sin, and that they might have matter for an evil report, that they might reproach me.* **14** *My God, think thou upon Tobiah and Sanballat according to these their works, and on the prophetess Noadiah, and the rest of the prophets, that would have put me in fear.*

Talk about a conspiracy! Shemaiah had been hired by the enemy, Tobiah and Sanballat! And to make matters worse, a prophetess named Noadiah and some other unnamed prophets were in on the plot!

And there is an interesting thing to learn from that. Women are every bit as capable as men of being dishonest, deceitful, and underhanded. Sin is not limited by gender! No one should ever be believed or disbelieved based on anatomy; truth should be sought for in every case, and assumptions should be left out entirely.

DO refuse to blindly trust or blithely distrust; verify, verify, verify!

Personal Notes:

_____
_____
_____
_____
_____
_____
_____
_____
_____
_____
_____
_____
_____
_____
_____
_____
_____
_____
_____
_____
_____
_____
_____
_____
_____
_____
_____

Devotion 81

The next verse we will consider brings us to a miracle of determination.

Nehemiah 6:15 *So the wall was finished in the twenty and fifth day of the month Elul, in fifty and two days.*

This was an amazing accomplishment! From a busted down wall lying in heaps of rubble, Nehemiah rallied the people, moved the rubble, and rebuilt the entire wall of the city in fifty-two days. With no power equipment, hydraulic tools, or diesel engines, working only by hand, they accomplished the task and did so with amazing speed.

And some things are going to have to be that way. When it comes to matters of life or death, the "governmental approach" (Okay, we need to put a bridge here; let's do forty years of study and then twenty years of construction!) is a horrible approach. So why do people do it that way? Mostly because they are more interested in giving themselves cover than they are in sticking out their neck...

Is sticking out your neck risky? Yes. Is due caution a good idea? Yes again. But most of the time, people are far more prone to the security of inactivity than they are to the risk of activity, when inactivity never actually changes anything!

That thing you know you need to be doing? DO it! No wall is ever going to build itself.

Personal Notes:

Devotion 82

The wall was now done, and the "fun" was about to truly begin.

Nehemiah 6:16 *And it came to pass, that when all our enemies heard thereof, and all the heathen that were about us saw these things, they were much cast down in their own eyes: for they perceived that this work was wrought of our God.*

There is a really weird, unbiblical mentality that seems to be taking root in our day—the idea that our main goal in life is to never offend, upset, or in any way disappoint the lost world around us. I see this very regularly in the weirdest, most unbelievable of ways. Every single day I begin my social media interaction with the world by posting a Bible verse, just a Bible verse, with no commentary on it at all. Almost invariably, someone feels compelled to comment underneath that verse as if I have done something wrong by posting it. Just yesterday, as I write this, I posted a verse, and immediately a man commented, "We must be careful about our expectations of the lost."

I did not post any expectations of the lost; I literally just posted a Bible verse. But you see, the commenter was recoiling in horror at the thought that someone in the lost world may read the actual words of Scripture and get upset!

I understand full well that sometimes "Christians" are incendiary and just plain stupid. That is not what I am talking about. I am talking about the fact that if we are determined to not offend the lost world, we will never do anything at all for God. Just by building a wall, Nehemiah managed to upset the lost world around him all the way into a depression! If you are more concerned about how the world feels than you are about how God feels, you will be utterly useless to God and the world both. In Nehemiah, the world saw a man who was determined to do a work for God, and they saw the power of God on him as he did. They may not have liked what they saw, but what they saw was a great testimony nonetheless.

DO be much more worried about offending God than you are about offending the lost world around you!

Personal Notes:

_____

_____

_____

_____

_____

_____

_____

_____

_____

_____

_____

_____

_____

_____

_____

_____

_____

_____

Devotion 83

We now arrive at one of the most maddening portions of the book of Nehemiah. For a bit of background, in case you have forgotten, there were several enemies in the book of Nehemiah. The main ones were Sanballat, Geshem, and Tobiah. Tobiah, in particular, was a man who used to be inside and then chose to be on the outside. Those three did everything they possibly could do to stop and destroy the work of God. They were enemies. They were enemies. They were enemies.

Did I mention that they were enemies? Ahem...

Nehemiah 6:17 *Moreover in those days the nobles of Judah sent many letters unto Tobiah, and the letters of Tobiah came unto them.* **18** *For there were many in Judah sworn unto him, because he was the son in law of Shechaniah the son of Arah; and his son Johanan had taken the daughter of Meshullam the son of Berechiah.* **19** *Also they reported his good deeds before me, and uttered my words to him. And Tobiah sent letters to put me in fear.*

Are you getting that? The people inside of the newly built walls, being protected and blessed by the newly built walls, were loyal to the people trying to destroy the walls instead of to the man and the people who built the walls! Tobiah was at that very moment actively fighting against Nehemiah, sending him threatening letters!

Read these words slowly and carefully and pay attention to the balance they describe. There are three kinds of people when it comes to a church. There are those who stay, there are those who leave, and there are those who leave and then actively try to destroy what they left. The first two, those who stay and those who leave, should be treated the same! They should be loved, prayed for, and wished well in all things. Some of my dearest friends in life to this day are people who once were members of my church and then decided it was not for them. They went elsewhere, have not caused us any trouble, and we still love each other as thoroughly as when they were still with us.

But that rare third, those who leave and then actively try to destroy what they left, should not be treated the same. They should be avoided like the plague.

DO avoid treating a non-enemy like a Tobiah, but DO also avoid treating a Tobiah like a non-enemy!

Personal Notes:

_____
_____
_____
_____
_____
_____
_____
_____
_____
_____
_____
_____
_____
_____

Devotion 84

As we arrive in chapter seven of the book of Nehemiah, the "adventure" part is laid aside for a bit, and the "paperwork" part is given. All of Nehemiah 7 is a genealogy of those who came back from captivity. It is nearly identical to the one recorded in Ezra 2. It has some slight differences because this one was taken fourteen years later, and families grow bigger or smaller during the years. But just prior to the long genealogy, we find Nehemiah setting some things in place for a particular reason.

Nehemiah 7:1 *Now it came to pass, when the wall was built, and I had set up the doors, and the porters and the singers and the Levites were appointed,* **2** *That I gave my brother Hanani, and Hananiah the ruler of the palace, charge over Jerusalem: for he was a faithful man, and feared God above many.* **3** *And I said unto them, Let not the gates of Jerusalem be opened until the sun be hot; and while they stand by, let them shut the doors, and bar them: and appoint watches of the inhabitants of Jerusalem, every one in his watch, and every one to be over against his house.* **4** *Now the city was large and great: but the people were few therein, and the houses were not builded.*

Nehemiah was preparing to go back to Persia for a time, as he had promised the king, and he, therefore, set his brother in charge over the affairs of the city. Hanani has been seen in the book before; he was the man who brought Nehemiah the report of how badly the people and the city were suffering.

Nehemiah's instructions were to keep the gates shut at night, for safety's sake, and to keep people on watch at all times. But why was the watch necessary when they had walls? Because walls are only as effective as the people manning them. Any unwatched walls will eventually be breached walls or broken walls!

No matter how well you have spiritual or practical "systems" set up in your life or home, DO stand watch over those systems!

Personal Notes:

_____
_____
_____
_____
_____
_____
_____
_____
_____
_____
_____
_____
_____
_____
_____
_____
_____
_____
_____
_____

Devotion 85

Chapter seven of the book of Nehemiah was a long chapter, seventy-three verses, and in it, Nehemiah took a genealogy and census of the people. And that brings us to chapter eight, which centers around an amazing eight-day revival.

Nehemiah 8:1 *And all the people gathered themselves together as one man into the street that was before the water gate; and they spake unto Ezra the scribe to bring the book of the law of Moses, which the LORD had commanded to Israel. 2 And Ezra the priest brought the law before the congregation both of men and women, and all that could hear with understanding, upon the first day of the seventh month. 3 And he read therein before the street that was before the water gate from the morning until midday, before the men and the women, and those that could understand; and the ears of all the people were attentive unto the book of the law.*

Ezra, the scribe, had been back for thirteen years now. I do not know how much preaching he did during those years, but I do know that he now received an invitation to do a city-wide crusade. People wanted something; they wanted to hear from the Bible. That is what God's real people always want.

In his message, the entire morning was spent just reading the text of Scripture. Depending on exactly how early they got started, we are looking at as much as six hours of plain Bible reading. To say that this message was "loaded with Bible" would be an understatement of epic proportions! And yet, there were no complaints about that because the people were hungry for it.

Our modern generation of "believers" far too many times seems to have a hunger for everything but this. "Give us emotional music, give us smoke, give us lights, give us anecdotes, give us inspirational pep talks!" Or, over on the other side of the tracks, "Give us blood and guts preaching, give us shouting and running the aisles, give us people getting 'saved' for the tenth time or more!"

And we wonder why there are "sides of the track" to begin with. Until all believers develop a hunger for Scripture above all else that life has to offer, we will continue to be just two sides of the same wobbly, spinning coin.

DO hunger for God's Word!

Personal Notes:

_____
_____
_____
_____
_____
_____
_____
_____
_____
_____
_____
_____
_____
_____

Devotion 86

As Nehemiah continued describing the beginning of the eight-day revival there in Jerusalem, we find mention of an interesting piece of furniture.

Nehemiah 8:4 *And Ezra the scribe stood upon a pulpit of wood, which they had made for the purpose; and beside him stood Mattithiah, and Shema, and Anaiah, and Urijah, and Hilkiah, and Maaseiah, on his right hand; and on his left hand, Pedaiah, and Mishael, and Malchiah, and Hashum, and Hashbadana, Zechariah, and Meshullam.*

This is the only mention of the pulpit in the Bible. It was something to elevate Ezra where he could be seen and heard. And once he was seen and heard, a beautiful sight ensued.

Nehemiah 8:5 *And Ezra opened the book in the sight of all the people; (for he was above all the people;) and when he opened it, all the people stood up:* **6** *And Ezra blessed the LORD, the great God. And all the people answered, Amen, Amen, with lifting up their hands: and they bowed their heads, and worshipped the LORD with their faces to the ground.*

When the Word of God was opened, everyone stood up out of respect. That is still a wonderful practice for today, especially since the Word of God is being given less respect than at any other time in human history. But in addition to that beautiful sight, we also find people saying amen and lifting up their hands and bowing their heads, and putting their faces on the ground to worship the Lord. This was clearly not a stuffy, dignified academic exercise; these people were truly engaged in worship.

DO leave formal, stuffy dignity to classroom biology lectures; our Lord deserves actual worship!

Personal Notes:

_____

_____

_____

_____

_____

_____

_____

_____

_____

_____

_____

_____

_____

_____

_____

_____

_____

_____

_____

_____

_____

_____

_____

_____

_____

Devotion 87

The next thing that Nehemiah describes for us in this eight-day revival is probably one of the most important things we should ever see and understand.

Nehemiah 8:8 *So they read in the book in the law of God distinctly, and gave the sense, and caused them to understand the reading.*

This verse explains what preaching is supposed to be all about. Read God's Word very clearly, give people the sense of it (meaning put it in words they can grasp), then cause them to understand it (meaning to be able to discern it and to apply it to their lives). When a preacher is done preaching a message, the people who have heard him ought to know what the Bible actually said, what those words actually mean, and how they are supposed to apply it in their own lives.

I have been in enough places to see two very opposite and yet equally horrible methodologies of preaching. On the one side is what I like to call "a triumph of scream over substance." It is entertaining to watch; fast, furious, and foolish. On the other side is what I like to call "vandalism by boredom." It is the dry, public parsing of every word while giving an in-depth discussion of every tense, mood, voice, and a thousand other aspects of every one of those publicly parsed words until everyone's eyes are crossing and even a lecture on the proper methodologies of a colonoscopy would seem exciting by contrast.

God's word is neither foolish nor boring, and it should never be served up as such. So whether you preach it or teach it or just discuss it with people, DO make it easy to understand and equally easy to apply!

Personal Notes:

_____

_____

_____

_____

_____

_____

_____

_____

_____

_____

_____

_____

_____

_____

_____

_____

_____

_____

_____

_____

_____

_____

_____

_____

_____

Devotion 88

As Ezra read and explained the Word of God to the people, a heartbreaking scene began to develop.

Nehemiah 8:9 *And Nehemiah, which is the Tirshatha* [That word means "governor"]*, and Ezra the priest the scribe, and the Levites that taught the people, said unto all the people, This day is holy unto the LORD your God; mourn not, nor weep. For all the people wept, when they heard the words of the law.*

If you have ever read the law of Moses going from Exodus through the book of Deuteronomy, then you can well understand why the people were crying as they listened to it being read and explained. It was all about the holy and righteous expectations of God for the people and the judgment that would come if His laws were violated.

Ezra was reading these words to people who were nowhere even close to keeping that law. In fact, it was even worse than that; due to their current situation, they were not able to even keep the entire law. And so they wept...

And Nehemiah and Ezra told them to stop.

Nehemiah 8:10 *Then he said unto them, Go your way, eat the fat, and drink the sweet, and send portions unto them for whom nothing is prepared: for this day is holy unto our Lord: neither be ye sorry; for the joy of the LORD is your strength.* **11** *So the Levites stilled all the people, saying, Hold your peace, for the day is holy; neither be ye grieved.* **12** *And all the people went their way to eat, and to drink, and to send* *portions, and to make great mirth, because they had understood the words that were declared unto them.*

It almost seems like an odd message to send, "No, you are not entirely perfect before God yet, but go be happy." What in the world is that? Simple; it was a recognition of how far they had come so very quickly and of the fact that they were willing to continue going that direction until they "arrived." These were not people who were living in rebellion against God; they were people who were spiritually growing by leaps and bounds and yet still had a way to go.

Sometimes we only see how far real Christians still have to go and refuse to take into account how far they have already come. DO avoid that mistake!

Personal Notes:

_____

_____

_____

_____

_____

_____

_____

_____

_____

_____

_____

_____

_____

_____

_____

_____

Devotion 89

The people there in Jerusalem had just come through a backbreaking building project. It would seem like the last thing anyone would want to do would be to build one more thing. But look at the very next thing that happened.

Nehemiah 8:13 *And on the second day were gathered together the chief of the fathers of all the people, the priests, and the Levites, unto Ezra the scribe, even to understand the words of the law.* **14** *And they found written in the law which the LORD had commanded by Moses, that the children of Israel should dwell in booths in the feast of the seventh month:* **15** *And that they should publish and proclaim in all their cities, and in Jerusalem, saying, Go forth unto the mount, and fetch olive branches, and pine branches, and myrtle branches, and palm branches, and branches of thick trees, to make booths, as it is written.* **16** *So the people went forth, and brought them, and made themselves booths, every one upon the roof of his house, and in their courts, and in the courts of the house of God, and in the street of the water gate, and in the street of the gate of Ephraim.* **17** *And all the congregation of them that were come again out of the captivity made booths, and sat under the booths: for since the days of Jeshua the son of Nun unto that day had not the children of Israel done so. And there was very great gladness.*

The verses they were reading were describing the Feast of Tabernacles, historically one of their most joyous feasts. It commemorated the time that God tabernacled with them for forty years in the wilderness. It seems as if on the very day this was to be taking place, they read in the Scripture and found out that it was to be taking place. It is amazing how timely the Word of God always is!

And so, realizing that they were supposed to be building booths, they went out and built booths, or as we would call them, tents.

If you are in the habit of reading God's Word, you will find that it not only gives you what you need, but it gives you WHAT you need WHEN you need it. So DO read it every day!

Personal Notes:

_____

_____

_____

_____

_____

_____

_____

_____

_____

_____

_____

_____

_____

_____

_____

_____

_____

_____

_____

Devotion 90

Here is a description of how the rest of the eight-day revival went for the people there in Jerusalem.

Nehemiah 8:18 *Also day by day, from the first day unto the last day, he read in the book of the law of God. And they kept the feast seven days; and on the eighth day was a solemn assembly, according unto the manner.*

Eight days of Bible reading. The people could not get enough of the Word of God! And on that day, they held what was called a solemn assembly. When we have read and absorbed the Word of God, it will cause some solemnity in our hearts. Interestingly, this was a scene of both gladness and solemnity at the same time. Those two things are not mutually exclusive. In fact, for a real child of God, when there is the realization that God and God's Word are working in our hearts, it will be both solemn and joyful at the exact same time.

All of this shows the immense power and value of the written Word of God. Just a couple of years ago, one of the most famous preachers in the world preached a message minimizing the written Word of God, especially the Old Testament. He was actually incredibly insulting to it. But it is evident that neither Nehemiah nor Ezra nor the people of God there in Jerusalem would have agreed with him.

DO love and value the written Word of God and the work that it does in your heart!

Personal Notes:

Devotion 91

In Nehemiah 8, the people had heard the words of the law read aloud, and they wept. Nehemiah and the priests, though, told them not to weep. God saw what they had just been through and the progress they had already made and was not angry with them. A time of rejoicing followed the seven days of the Feast of Tabernacles, followed by the eighth day, often called the great day of the feast. Chapter nine begins on the very next day.

Nehemiah 9:1 *Now in the twenty and fourth day of this month the children of Israel were assembled with fasting, and with sackclothes, and earth upon them. 2 And the seed of Israel separated themselves from all strangers, and stood and confessed their sins, and the iniquities of their fathers. 3 And they stood up in their place, and read in the book of the law of the LORD their God one fourth part of the day; and another fourth part they confessed, and worshipped the LORD their God.*

After rejoicing and after enjoying their relationship with the God of Israel, the people were then ready to actually deal with their sin. Now be honest; does that not sound completely backward to us? Even in Scripture, the normal pattern is that wayward believers get under conviction and repent and start walking on the right path and then experience the joy of restoration.

But the issue in that last sentence is the word "normal." You see, we get very used to normal, so much so that we often come to think of it as "always."

But God knows each and every situation of each and every person far better than we do, and if He chooses to put the cart of joy before the horse of "getting everything just right," He has every right to do so! And especially with people who are actually intent on getting everything right, as those in Jerusalem clearly were, God is often way more patient and way more "giving" than we would be.

DO remember that if God ever puts the cart before the horse, the cart will actually pull the horse!

Personal Notes:

_____
_____
_____
_____
_____
_____
_____
_____
_____
_____
_____
_____
_____
_____
_____
_____
_____
_____
_____

Devotion 92

In Nehemiah 9:2, we saw the people weeping and repenting of their sin. In verse three, we learned that they then stood up, read the Bible for a fourth of the day, confessed their sins for another fourth of the day, and worshipped the Lord.

And then we come to two verses of Scripture that are either beautiful or disconcerting depending on your view of God and of your own "dignity."

Nehemiah 9:4 *Then stood up upon the stairs, of the Levites, Jeshua, and Bani, Kadmiel, Shebaniah, Bunni, Sherebiah, Bani, and Chenani, and cried with a loud voice unto the LORD their God. 5 Then the Levites, Jeshua, and Kadmiel, Bani, Hashabniah, Sherebiah, Hodijah, Shebaniah, and Pethahiah, said, Stand up and bless the LORD your God for ever and ever: and blessed be thy glorious name, which is exalted above all blessing and praise.*

Simply put, these Levites, ministers and members of the clergy, stood up and shouted praise to God at the top of their lungs. Then they told everyone else to stand up and do the same thing. Can you imagine this? These "carnal," emotional Levites instructed the people to stand up and bless the Lord. Why, someone should have turned off their microphones, made them leave the platform at once, and then calmed everybody down!

I remember sitting in a Bible college chapel many years ago on a day when a young man in the student body shouted, "Glory to God!" during the service. It was not showy or done at some inappropriate time; it was right in the middle of "worship." And yet the next thing that caught my attention was a faculty member seated on the platform staring at the young man and pulling his finger across his throat in the throat-cutting gesture meant to say, "Cut that out right now."

I rather suspect Dr. Dignity would not have been very comfortable there in Jerusalem on the day we are reading about in our text.

Do we or do we not have a God who is worthy of praise? Has God or has He not been incredibly good to all of us? If the answer to those questions is yes (and it obviously is), then shouting His praises is a perfectly reasonable and logical thing to do.

DO shout His praises!

Personal Notes:

_____
_____
_____
_____
_____
_____
_____
_____
_____
_____
_____
_____
_____
_____
_____

Devotion 93

In yesterday's devotion, we observed that the Levites shouted the praises of God and then got everyone else to do so as well. But, as with most everything in Scripture, it will not take us long to see the other side of the coin. In fact, the rest of the chapter IS the other side of the coin.

Here is what I mean. We flawed humans have a remarkable ability to get things wrong even while trying to get things right. And the arena of praise and worship is no exception. For every living corpse who would not so much as crack a smile if Jesus Himself were preaching and the entire heavenly choir was singing, there is a wild-eyed praise addict who worships worship while imagining that he is worshipping the Lord. I have been in far too many services in far too many places where people were shouting and either had no idea why or were actually shouting over something that definitely did not deserve to be shouted over!

But from verse six to verse thirty-eight, every single verse gives some practical or theological reason to actually be engaging in praise! It starts with creation in verse six:

Nehemiah 9:6 *Thou, even thou, art LORD alone; thou hast made heaven, the heaven of heavens, with all their host, the earth, and all things that are therein, the seas, and all that is therein, and thou preservest them all; and the host of heaven worshippeth thee.*

Then in verse seven, it covers the Abrahamic covenant; in verses nine through eleven, it covers the miraculous exodus from Egypt, including the miracle of the parting of the Red Sea; in verse twelve, it praises Him for the pillar of fire by night and pillar of cloud by day that He led them with; in verse thirteen it gives Him glory for the giving of the Ten Commandments, and it just keeps on going like that until the end of the chapter.

Should we shout and praise God? Yes. But rather than just shouting to be shouting, or shouting because others are shouting, or shouting because someone has told you that you should be shouting, DO learn about our God and His goodness, and then shout about that!

Personal Notes:

_____

_____

_____

_____

_____

_____

_____

_____

_____

_____

_____

_____

_____

_____

_____

Devotion 94

In the very last verse of chapter nine, the last thing the Levites said in their praise to God was, "And because of all this we make a sure covenant, and write it; and our princes, Levites, and priests, seal unto it."

But we are not just told that they made a covenant and signed their names to it; in chapter ten, we are actually given the text of that covenant. Verses one through twenty-seven give us the names of the people who put their names on the line, and verses twenty-eight and following tell us what they signed to. Let's just look at a few verses of that covenant:

Nehemiah 10:29 *They clave to their brethren, their nobles, and entered into a curse, and into an oath, to walk in God's law, which was given by Moses the servant of God, and to observe and do all the commandments of the LORD our Lord, and his judgments and his statutes;* **30** *And that we would not give our daughters unto the people of the land, nor take their daughters for our sons:* **31** *And if the people of the land bring ware or any victuals on the sabbath day to sell, that we would not buy it of them on the sabbath, or on the holy day: and that we would leave the seventh year, and the exaction of every debt.* **32** *Also we made ordinances for us, to charge ourselves yearly with the third part of a shekel for the service of the house of our God;* **33** *For the shewbread, and for the continual meat offering, and for the continual burnt offering, of the sabbaths, of the new moons, for the set feasts, and for the holy things, and for the sin* *offerings to make an atonement for Israel, and for all the work of the house of our God.*

In these verses, they committed to obeying the Mosaic law, refusing to allow their children to intermarry with the lost heathens around them, keeping God's Day holy, handling their brethren's debts the way God commanded, and properly financing the work of God's House.

Even without the remaining verses, that is an impressive list! But the most impressive thing about it is that they did not just say it; they put it in writing. Can you even imagine the uproar today if a preacher preached a message covering such a wide range of big things and then said, "Now, before you go today, I have written out contracts for all of you to sign, agreeing to abide by all of this!"

We are not going to do that. But our commitment to doing right should be as firm as if we did! Don't just hear God's Word; in your heart, DO put it in contract form and then sign your name to it!

Personal Notes:

_____
_____
_____
_____
_____
_____
_____
_____
_____
_____

Devotion 95

As we come to Nehemiah 11, the first two verses give us a "Wait, what?" moment.

Nehemiah 11:1 *And the rulers of the people dwelt at Jerusalem: the rest of the people also cast lots, to bring one of ten to dwell in Jerusalem the holy city, and nine parts to dwell in other cities. 2 And the people blessed all the men, that willingly offered themselves to dwell at Jerusalem.*

The most prized piece of real estate on earth today is Jerusalem. It was like that during the days of David and Solomon and the entire monarchy of Judah, too. So when we read that people were drawing straws to see who had to live there and that people were praising whoever agreed to do so if their lot was drawn, it lets us know that something was very different in those days.

And it was. Remember that just a few months earlier, the city was in ruins, the wall was lying in heaps of rubble, and only a handful of people were brave enough to live there. And even once the wall was completed, there was no throne and no king. But what there was plenty of was enemies who wanted to kill whoever lived there and tear the walls down again. So in those days, living in Jerusalem was a sacrifice and an act of valor! But those who did so became the foundation that future generations built on. And by the time of Christ, Jerusalem was once again the chief joy of the nation.

Anyone can stroll into an established situation. But those with the courage to build something for others who will come after them deserve the praise that "Easy Street believers" never really earn. Mind you, there is nothing sinful about walking into a situation where everything is already perfect... but there is nothing noteworthy about it either. DO be willing to build for those who will come after you!

Personal Notes:

_____

_____

_____

_____

_____

_____

_____

_____

_____

_____

_____

_____

_____

_____

_____

_____

_____

_____

_____

_____

_____

_____

_____

_____

Devotion 96

In the first two verses of Nehemiah 11, we saw people volunteering for the very difficult task of living in Jerusalem in the days after the return from captivity. The rest of the chapter will give us a list of those who volunteered to do so. And there are some very constructive things to find in that list.

Nehemiah 11:4 *And at Jerusalem dwelt certain of the children of Judah, and of the children of Benjamin. Of the children of Judah; Athaiah the son of Uzziah, the son of Zechariah, the son of Amariah, the son of Shephatiah, the son of Mahalaleel, of the children of Perez;* **5** *And Maaseiah the son of Baruch, the son of Colhozeh, the son of Hazaiah, the son of Adaiah, the son of Joiarib, the son of Zechariah, the son of Shiloni.* **6** *All the sons of Perez that dwelt at Jerusalem were four hundred threescore and eight valiant men.*

Perez, elsewhere called Pharez, had 468 of his male descendants living in the city, and all of them were recorded as being valiant, brave men. Let that sink in; out of 468 boys and men, there was not a coward among them. Just on a statistical basis alone, that is absolutely incredible!

You have perhaps noticed that "manhood" in our day and in our land seems to have fallen on some very hard times. For many decades now, there has been a concerted, intentional effort to feminize boys and men. That effort comes directly from the twisted head and filthy heart of the devil himself, who hates any design of God. The Bible tells us that in the beginning, God made them male and female. Throughout the Scripture, men are repeatedly commanded to be brave and not to fear. Throughout the Scripture, men were praised for strength and valor. Nowhere in Scripture was femininity or timidity regarded as a good thing in a man.

In Nehemiah's day, without hundreds of brave men and boys, no one in the city would ever survive. The walls stood and the city was rebuilt and Christ and the apostles had a city of Jerusalem to minister in because men in hard times were actually manly.

Parents, DO teach your boys to be manly, strong, valiant, and brave. Teach them not to be cowards. Teach them to be willing to fight when necessary. In other words, DO teach them to be what God created them to be!

Personal Notes:

_____

_____

_____

_____

_____

_____

_____

_____

_____

_____

_____

_____

_____

_____

Devotion 97

As chapter twelve of the book of Nehemiah begins, the list of warriors and workers in Jerusalem that chapter eleven gave us is now done, and a different type of list begins to be given.

Nehemiah 12:1 *Now these are the priests and the Levites that went up with Zerubbabel the son of Shealtiel, and Jeshua: Seraiah, Jeremiah, Ezra,* **2** *Amariah, Malluch, Hattush,* **3** *Shechaniah, Rehum, Meremoth,* **4** *Iddo, Ginnetho, Abijah,* **5** *Miamin, Maadiah, Bilgah,* **6** *Shemaiah, and Joiarib, Jedaiah,* **7** *Sallu, Amok, Hilkiah, Jedaiah. These were the chief of the priests and of their brethren in the days of Jeshua.*

These verses give us the names of the main priests that came from Babylon back to Jerusalem many years previous under Zerubbabel, Ezra included among them. But why, in a book about a construction project, would a list of priests and Levites be given? Simply because walls would be of no use without worship...

It was not a lack of construction workers or a lack of soldiers that caused the walls to be knocked down to begin with; it was people who turned away from following God. And these brand-new walls would be no better than the old walls if that did not change.

It is very easy to place our faith in military strength or in personal strength or in financial strength or in mental strength. But when have those things ever kept a corrupt family or church or nation from falling?

History is littered with the wreckage of once nearly all-powerful empires that rotted from the inside out.

DO make worship your primary purpose in life; no walls that you ever build can long stand without it.

Personal Notes:

_____
_____
_____
_____
_____
_____
_____
_____
_____
_____
_____
_____
_____
_____
_____
_____
_____
_____
_____
_____
_____
_____
_____

Devotion 98

When we read all of Nehemiah 12, the verses give us a description of the people being divided into two large companies, walking up on the walls and praising the Lord while facing each other. But three of the verses give us a bit of a time element to that arrangement as well:

Nehemiah 12:24 *And the chief of the Levites: Hashabiah, Sherebiah, and Jeshua the son of Kadmiel, with their brethren over against them, to praise and to give thanks, according to the commandment of David the man of God, ward over against ward.* **25** *Mattaniah, and Bakbukiah, Obadiah, Meshullam, Talmon, Akkub, were porters keeping the ward at the thresholds of the gates.* **26** *These were in the days of Joiakim the son of Jeshua, the son of Jozadak, and in the days of Nehemiah the governor, and of Ezra the priest, the scribe.*

The fact that this arrangement took place all during the years of Joiakim, Nehemiah, and Ezra, lets us know that it lasted for decades. This was not a haphazard or random thing. It was an acknowledgment that worshipping God was worthy of being "put on the schedule and kept there." And this had been originally instituted hundreds of years earlier under the direction of David, the man after God's own heart!

If it seems like God is very much pleased with being praised and thanked, it is because He is.

Here in America, we have Thanksgiving DAY. Day...

DO make EVERY day of your life a day of thanks and praise to God!

Personal Notes:

_____

_____

_____

_____

_____

_____

_____

_____

_____

_____

_____

_____

_____

_____

_____

_____

_____

_____

_____

_____

_____

_____

_____

_____

_____

_____

_____

_____

_____

_____

Devotion 99

Things had come very far since God placed a burden upon one man's heart to go and rebuild the walls of Jerusalem. Nehemiah had come from Persia, set to the task, rallied the people, defended the work against enemies within and without, called for a revival, and accomplished all that he set his hand to do. The walls were now built, and the city was fully functioning. Happily ever after, right?

If you think that, you do not know either the devil or human nature...

Nehemiah 13:1 *On that day they read in the book of Moses in the audience of the people; and therein was found written, that the Ammonite and the Moabite should not come into the congregation of God for ever;* **2** *Because they met not the children of Israel with bread and with water, but hired Balaam against them, that he should curse them: howbeit our God turned the curse into a blessing.* **3** *Now it came to pass, when they had heard the law, that they separated from Israel all the mixed multitude.*

More than a thousand years before Nehemiah's day, the Ammonites and the Moabites had tried their absolute best to wipe Israel out. And God vowed to never forget that. He went so far as to forbid an Ammonite or Moabite from coming into the congregation of God forever. Mind you, when individual Ammonites or Moabites, such as Ruth, came to know Him, they became proselytes of Israel and ceased to be regarded as Ammonites or Moabites.

But this otherwise wholesale prohibition was given by the God who knew that the Ammonites and Moabites would always and forever be the enemies of Israel and caused them innumerable problems. And yet, in spite of that, in Nehemiah's day, it was discovered that Ammonites were in the midst of the congregation.

Problems from without are bad enough; problems from within are absolutely lethal. The good news is that, in this case, the people had enough spiritual wherewithal to do right once they recognized the problem.

DO take stock of your "inner circle." If you have allowed spiritual Ammonites in that circle, it is time to remove them!

Personal Notes:

_____

_____

_____

_____

_____

_____

_____

_____

_____

_____

_____

_____

_____

_____

_____

_____

Devotion 100

Not only did the children of Israel have Ammonite problems, we quickly find that they had a very serious problem with a very specific Ammonite.

Nehemiah 13:4 *And before this, Eliashib the priest, having the oversight of the chamber of the house of our God, was allied unto Tobiah:* **5** *And he had prepared for him a great chamber, where aforetime they laid the meat offerings, the frankincense, and the vessels, and the tithes of the corn, the new wine, and the oil, which was commanded to be given to the Levites, and the singers, and the porters; and the offerings of the priests.*

There is that Tobiah guy again, an Ammonite and the enemy that caused Nehemiah and the people of God problems throughout the entire book. But the real problem is that Eliashib, the priest, had actually made this enemy an apartment in the house of God! And, making matters infinitely worse, Nehemiah 3:1 tells us that Eliashib was not just any average priest; he was actually the high priest!

Had he done much good? Certainly, he was actually one of the builders of the wall, having worked on the Sheep Gate. But "doing some good" is never going to get anyone a free pass to take the enemies of God by the hand, bring them into the midst of the sheep, and turn them loose like a hungry wolf.

DO think enough of the sheep to never serve them up to the wolves!

Personal Notes:

_____
_____
_____
_____
_____
_____
_____
_____
_____
_____
_____
_____
_____
_____
_____
_____
_____
_____
_____
_____
_____
_____
_____
_____
_____
_____
_____
_____

Devotion 101

Eliashib, the high priest, had made an apartment in the very House of God for Tobiah, who had spent all day every day for years opposing the work of God. But as we look at the very next verse, we learn why that was able to happen to begin with.

Nehemiah 13:6 *But in all this time was not I at Jerusalem: for in the two and thirtieth year of Artaxerxes king of Babylon came I unto the king, and after certain days obtained I leave of the king: 7 And I came to Jerusalem, and understood of the evil that Eliashib did for Tobiah, in preparing him a chamber in the courts of the house of God.*

You should be able to easily finish this statement: when the cat's away...

But Nehemiah was not fond of mice. Or of rats, in the case of Eliashib and Tobiah. Boy, was he EVER not fond of them:

Nehemiah 13:8 *And it grieved me sore: therefore I cast forth all the household stuff of Tobiah out of the chamber.*

To me, this is far and away, the funniest passage in the Bible. Can you imagine the conversation between Nehemiah and some of his more "diplomatic" associates?

"Now, Nehemiah, I understand that you are a wee bit upset about the Ammonite in the temple. But everyone is welcome here, even if they are here to cause trouble…"

CLANG! BANG CLANK CLANK CLANK!

"You need to stop. If you keep throwing his stuff out, you may hurt his feelings!"

HEAVE! WHOOSH BANG CLANG CLANK CLANK!

Epic, absolutely epic! But also absolutely necessary since Tobiah was a certified wolf. DO be willing to place the welfare of the sheep above the feelings of the wolves!

Personal Notes:

_____

_____

_____

_____

_____

_____

_____

_____

_____

_____

_____

_____

_____

_____

_____

_____

_____

_____

_____

_____

_____

_____

Devotion 102

As Nehemiah continued to survey the problems that had developed while he was away in Persia, here is another issue that he found.

Nehemiah 13:15 *In those days saw I in Judah some treading wine presses on the sabbath, and bringing in sheaves, and lading asses; as also wine, grapes, and figs, and all manner of burdens, which they brought into Jerusalem on the sabbath day: and I testified against them in the day wherein they sold victuals.*

People have a pretty bad habit of making promises and then simply forgetting about them. Nehemiah saw people running their businesses wide open on the Sabbath day. It was contrary to the law. It was also completely the opposite of what all of them had promised just a few years before:

Nehemiah 10:29 *They clave to their brethren, their nobles, and entered into a curse, and into an oath, to walk in God's law, which was given by Moses the servant of God, and to observe and do all the commandments of the LORD our Lord, and his judgments and his statutes;* **30** *And that we would not give our daughters unto the people of the land, nor take their daughters for our sons:* **31** *And if the people of the land bring ware or any victuals on the sabbath day to sell, that we would not buy it of them on the sabbath, or on the holy day: and that we would leave the seventh year, and the exaction of every debt.*

Promise? What promise? We don't remember any promise…

"I will be faithful! I will tithe! I will serve! In fact, Preacher, anything you need me to do, I will be there for it! I am looking for Jesus to come, and I want to be in the center of His will when He does!"

What promise, indeed.

Anyone can vow to do right. But the unfulfilled vow of a Christian is not one bit better than the empty campaign promises of a sleazy politician. DO what you are supposed to do, and especially DO what you have said you will do!

Personal Notes:

_____

_____

_____

_____

_____

_____

_____

_____

_____

_____

_____

_____

_____

_____

_____

_____

_____

_____

_____

_____

Devotion 103

As Nehemiah took steps to correct the issue of people violating the Sabbath, we find another hilarious instance of his *ahem* untactfulness.

Nehemiah 13:16 *There dwelt men of Tyre also therein, which brought fish, and all manner of ware, and sold on the sabbath unto the children of Judah, and in Jerusalem.* **17** *Then I contended with the nobles of Judah, and said unto them, What evil thing is this that ye do, and profane the sabbath day?* **18** *Did not your fathers thus, and did not our God bring all this evil upon us, and upon this city? yet ye bring more wrath upon Israel by profaning the sabbath.* **19** *And it came to pass, that when the gates of Jerusalem began to be dark before the sabbath, I commanded that the gates should be shut, and charged that they should not be opened till after the sabbath: and some of my servants set I at the gates, that there should no burden be brought in on the sabbath day.* **20** *So the merchants and sellers of all kind of ware lodged without Jerusalem once or twice.* **21** *Then I testified against them, and said unto them, Why lodge ye about the wall? if ye do so again, I will lay hands on you. From that time forth came they no more on the sabbath.*

Merchants trying to make their way into Jerusalem on the Sabbath found the gates locked. So they simply camped out around the wall, hoping to still find a way to make a buck. At which point Nehemiah threatened to "lay hands on them."

He meant that very literally. He actually threatened to beat them up!

Now, for the record, it is, generally speaking, not usually the best idea for the testimony to be threatening to throw hands. But in this case, it was completely necessary and did the job very thoroughly. The point is, Nehemiah was willing to do much more than just talk about the problem. If all we are ever willing to do is "have a conversation" about things that are wrong, then those wrong things will simply continue to happen forever.

DO be willing to take a firm stand against sin!

Personal Notes:

_____

_____

_____

_____

_____

_____

_____

_____

_____

_____

_____

_____

_____

_____

_____

_____

_____

_____

Devotion 104

The problems that had arisen while Nehemiah was gone just continued to bubble to the surface. And the next one was truly, horribly bad.

Nehemiah 13:23 *In those days also saw I Jews that had married wives of Ashdod, of Ammon, and of Moab: 24 And their children spake half in the speech of Ashdod, and could not speak in the Jews' language, but according to the language of each people.*

These Jewish men made the same mistake as Solomon by marrying foreign, unbelieving women. Those women then raised their children speaking in their mother's native tongue. Half of the kids could speak the language of Ashdod, but none could speak Hebrew. And, as always, this was not an issue of race or skin; it was an issue of sin. Since these children could not understand Hebrew, they could not be told about the God of the Hebrews. So not only would they almost certainly not come to know God, they would also influence others away from Him as well.

Children were now going to be caught in the crosshairs thanks to the disobedience of the adults.

Adults would do well to remember that what we do affects the lives of the generation coming up behind us. And this is one reason why God, even in the New Testament, told us not to be unequally yoked with unbelievers.

DO marry right, and DO raise the children right!

Personal Notes:

Devotion 105

In yesterday's devotion, we saw Nehemiah becoming aware of the huge problem of Jewish men having intermarried with heathen women, who were then raising their children in their heathen ways in the midst of God's congregation. And, as we have already learned about Nehemiah, "tactfulness" was not exactly his strong suit...

Nehemiah 13:25 *And I contended with them, and cursed them* [this does not mean he uttered profanities, it means he pronounced dose of judgment against them], *and smote certain of them, and plucked off their hair, and made them swear by God, saying, Ye shall not give your daughters unto their sons, nor take their daughters unto your sons, or for yourselves.*

Are you getting that? Nehemiah literally slapped people around and ripped the hair off of their heads.

Repeat after me, "My pastor is really a fairly nice guy!"

In all seriousness, this demonstrates once again how vile it is in the sight of God for a believer to ever marry a nonbeliever. He has never changed his mind on this and never will.

DO hold the line on this; it is never God's will for a believer to marry a nonbeliever!

Personal Notes:

Devotion 106

There was one last problem that Nehemiah had to deal with, and (not surprisingly) he did.

Nehemiah 13:28 *And one of the sons of Joiada, the son of Eliashib the high priest, was son in law to Sanballat the Horonite: therefore I chased him from me.*

Let me give you commentator Adam Clarke's take on this verse, if for no other reason, just because of the word he uses, which, I've decided, is quite possibly the coolest word of all times:

"Those who set at open defiance the laws of God and man, and whose continued presence is inconsistent with the welfare of the community, should not be permitted to live in it; and in all wise and good efforts to prevent their pestiferous influence, men may expect the aid of the enlightened, patriotic, and good, and the blessing of God."

Pestiferous... you have to admit, that is a very cool word. And it is not hard to figure out when you see that the first four letters make up the word "pest."

Nehemiah was very careful to consider the influence people were going to have. And whenever he found someone who was going to defy the very laws of God and actively convince others to do so, he got rid of him. Mind you, there is a very big difference between people who simply have honest disagreements and someone who is determined to draw people into sin. And as kindhearted as we always wish we could be, there will be the occasional rare circumstance in which we are actually dealing with a devil in the flesh who is determined to draw people into sin, and we will not be able to "be nice" to that person any more than a parent would be "nice" to the pervert trying to lure their child into a van with a promise of candy.

DO be willing to be a spiritual "mama bear" when it is needed!

Personal Notes:

_____
_____
_____
_____
_____
_____
_____
_____
_____
_____
_____
_____
_____
_____
_____
_____
_____
_____
_____
_____
_____
_____
_____

Devotion 107

After spending years of his life and vast sums of his fortune to rebuild the wall and to set things right in Jerusalem, after battling enemies without and within, Nehemiah closed out the book with a plea from the heart that all of us should have coming from our hearts as well.

Nehemiah 13:29 *Remember them, O my God, because they have defiled the priesthood, and the covenant of the priesthood, and of the Levites.* **30** *Thus cleansed I them from all strangers, and appointed the wards of the priests and the Levites, every one in his business;* **31** *And for the wood offering, at times appointed, and for the firstfruits. Remember me, O my God, for good.*

Remember me, O my God, for good…

May I paraphrase that, please? "God, I have done my very best. I have laid it all on the line, I have made people angry when it was necessary, I have labored night and day, I have followed your Word, and I am not ashamed to ask you to please remember me, for good."

Stop and think about that. When it comes to God, do most people want Him to remember or to forget? Clearly, most of us want Him to forget! And there will always be an aspect of that that is true. We all definitely want God to choose to forget our sins, as He has promised to do. But if that is all we are ever able to ask for, then, with all due respect, "we are doing it wrong."

Yes, salvation is completely the free gift of God based on what Jesus did on Calvary. But after we are saved, we still have a life that we live in which we make choices every single day. Choices to obey or disobey. Choices to be faithful or unfaithful. Choices to be a good influence or a bad influence. And if we are not able to ask God to please remember what we have done and are doing, then we need to change what we are doing.

DO live your life in such a way that you are not embarrassed to ask God to please remember!

Personal Notes:

_____
_____
_____
_____
_____
_____
_____
_____
_____
_____
_____
_____
_____
_____
_____
_____
_____
_____
_____
_____

The Night Heroes Series

Cry from the Coal Mine (Vol 1)
Free Fall (Vol 2)
Broken Brotherhood (Vol 3)
The Blade of Black Crow (Vol 4)
Ghost Ship (Vol 5)
When Serpents Rise (Vol 6)
Moth Man (Vol 7)
Runaway (Vol 8)
Terror by Day (Vol 9)
Winter Wolf (Vol 10)
Desert Heat (Vol 11)

Other Fiction

Zak Blue: Falcon Wing
Zak Blue: Enter the Maelstrom

Other Books by Dr. Wagner

Daniel: Breathtaking
Esther: Five Feasts and the Fingerprints of God
Galatians: The Treasure of Liberty
James: The Pen and the Plumb Line
Jonah: A Story of Greatness
Nehemiah: A Labor of Love
Proverbs Vol 1: Bright Light from Dark Sayings
Proverbs Vol 2: Bright Light from Dark Sayings
The Revelation: Ready or Not
Romans: Salvation from A-Z
Ruth: Diamonds in the Darkness

Beyond the Colored Coat
From Footers to Finish Nails
Learning Not to Fear the Old Testament
Marriage Makers/Marriage Breakers
I'm Saved! Now What???
Don't Muzzle the Ox

Devotionals

DO Drops Vol. 1
DO Drops Vol. 2
DO Drops Vol. 3
DO Drops Vol. 4
DO Drops Vol. 5
DO Drops Vol. 6
DO Drops Vol. 7
DO Drops Vol. 8
DO Drops Vol. 9